DITCH  GLITCH

WITH Kate EMMERSON

www.metzpress.co.za

Join Kate's communities of support and inspiration

I have created a unique, private Facebook group for you. Once your request to join it has been approved, you'll be able to share your inspirational stories, insights and trials, get expert help from Kate and be supported by others on a similar journey. This group will help you to ditch your glitch and shift your life so that you can live light, live large.

To join the group, mail my team on shift@kate-emmerson.com and put "Request to join ditch it" in the subject line. I will also send you all of the worksheets contained in the book.

There are plenty of ways to stay in touch with me:
www.facebook.com/kate-emmerson.page
www.kate-emmerson.com
Twitter: @kate_emmerson
LinkedIn: www.linkedin.com/in/kateemmerson

Published in 2015 by
Metz Press
1 Cameronians Avenue
Welgemoed, 7530
South Africa

Copyright © Metz Press 2017
Text copyright © Kate Emmerson

All rights reserved. No part of this publication may be reproduced, stored in a retrieval system or transmitted in any form or by any means, electronic, mechanical, photocopying, recording or otherwise, without the prior written permission of the copyright owners.

Publisher: Wilsia Metz
Copy editor: Susie Dinneen
Cover photography: Piet Filmalter
Cover design concept: Adrian Lombard and Essential Earth Global team
Designer: Liezl Maree
Proofreader: Hanneke Gagiano

POD ISBN: 978-1-928376-28-6
PRINT ISBN: 978-1-928376-28-6
EPUB ISBN: 978-1-928376-26-2

DEDICATION

This book is for my beautiful,
courageous mom and my inspirational,
entrepreneurial dad. Thank you both for
sharing a part of you with me.
With love, K

Foreword

Kate Emmerson is the product of glitches ditched. I can think of no one better to bring others through this challenging journey. In my 20 years of practice, I have witnessed patients wrestle with self-limiting, fear-based beliefs, which rob them of the elegance of success. While each of us is capable of fleeting victories, that glitch is a scythe to success, chopping us off at the knees each time we venture beyond our self-imposed limitations.

My journey as a keen observer, friend and exponent of Kate's has allowed me to witness her metamorphosis as she's ditched her own glitches. Starting out in practice as a young homeopath and acupuncturist, I shared an office with Kate. Her effervescent personality and client-centric attitude engender instant magnetism, which is portrayed in her writing. It is this same client-centric altruism that allows her to bare her own story, revealing her vulnerability. It is never easy to expose your own issues as an example for others to learn from, which epitomises her passion and dedication to her audience.

The true value of this book is that Kate's teaching, combined with her vulnerability, gives her inimitable authority. Her authority in her subject and teaching stems from her ability to own her "stuff" without apology or excuse. However, do not be lulled by her altruism and care, as she demands stringent commitment to shifting, with definite ferocity.

Many self-help books make a great read and are more a theoretical treatise than practical tool. I have seen my fair share of self-help book junkies, who use their latest read as a temporary salve to massage into their emotional wounds and ease their pain as long as they are between its covers. *Ditch your Glitch,* you can be sure, is going to challenge you to effect long-overdue changes. Finally, you can jettison the corrosive self-limitations that hamper the cogs of your success machine. Kate will support you in this arduous journey, while you learn skills that are forgiving, boundary creating, un-limiting and not fear based.

Dr Colin La Grange
Registered Doctor of Chinese Medicine, Acupuncturist and Homeopath

Acknowledgements

There are times when I THINK that the process of writing a book is profoundly simple – you have an idea, you sit your bum on your chair, and you type, type, type. Then some time later, voilà, a manuscript is complete and that becomes a book on a shelf. Simple!

Then there are times when I let myself FEEL that it is the most profoundly difficult journey one can willingly undertake. We need to become someone different in the conception, creation and completion of a book. I needed way more support for this book than for my first one, which I wrote two years ago. Gremlins abounded and confounded me at every turn – "will this book be as well-received as my first?", "what if I have nothing life-changing to say?" – and all the rest of the self-belittling jabber we tell ourselves. The irony is that it is the exact topic contained in these pages, so I was able to use the practical exercises in this book to re-work through my own stuff. Then I just let myself write, stick to deadlines, re-write, re-work, take out, find new, panic, breathe, laugh, cry, get angry, dislike the manuscript, love the manuscript. Complicated!

In a flash of inspiration (perhaps desperation) I created a mastermind group of other writers who wanted to complete a book too. That wonderful journey has accompanied the pulling together and writing of this book. I am indebted to each of you for your support and bravery in tackling your own manuscripts and sharing "bum time" with me, as we fondly call it. Your support kept me going, and I was constantly inspired by your stories.

I also wish to acknowledge all my family and teachers in life, who demand that I stretch myself. Whether your influence on me has appeared outwardly as positive or negative, it has undoubtedly shaped my life to what it is today. A life I love!

I acknowledge every single person I have ever met. When I write, a word, a sentence or an idea will often bring up spontaneous flashbacks to moments on my journey in life. They could be once-off interactions: meeting a person after a talk, a smile to a stranger on the subway, watching someone on a street corner. Sometimes they're from my life-long relationship with my family, a best friend, my soul sister, people who were once my friends, my challengers and prodders, or colleagues. These flashbacks give me a glimpse of who I am and what I still have left to do on my path.

To all my clients who have dared to allow me to enter your lives and who share stories here to inspire others with your courage: Bless you for doing the work. You are brave and inspirational.

A massive thank you to my very supportive friends, clients and colleagues who helped me crowd-fund another special project that happened simultaneously to this book. Your support and belief in me helped to bring my energy back to this book with ease.

My life is full and beautiful, even when there are tears to process and potatoes to bash, and for that I thank YOU, yes, YOU.

Contents

INTRODUCTION   9
The process   19
Commitment   20
Your toolkit   23
Your daily ritual   24

PART 1: STEPPING IN   29
Step 1: Take stock of your life   30
Step 2: Dare to ask   34
Step 3: Find a different perspective   36
Step 4: Get to grips with your glitch   37

PART 2: STEPPING UP   50
Step 5: Envision your future   51
Step 6: Ignite your cycle of life   55
Step 7: Remind yourself   60
Step 8: Get jiggy with your goals   61
Step 9: Make an action plan   62
Step 10: Find your self-limiting beliefs   65
Step 11: Limit your self-limiting beliefs   70
Step 12: Lug your load   77
Let's pause   80
Step 13: Set ballsy boundaries   82
Step 14: Live your values   87
Step 15: Take action   92
Step 16: Forgive and be free   96
Time to reflect   103
Step 17: Clear your clutter   105
Step 18: Boost your bucket before you kick the bucket!   110
Step 19: Face your false fears   113
Step 20: Pull out all the stops   119

PART 3: STEPPING OUT   123
Step 21: Shine your light   123
Healing modalities   129
Stay connected: support for your journey   136

More client inspiration to support your journey of transformation   139
Diagrams and worksheets   146
Further reading   158
Reviews   159

"There is only one thing that makes a dream impossible to achieve: the fear of failure."
Paulo Coelho, *The Alchemist*

Introduction

When you are ready to make changes, it can be useful to have someone who sees your highest potential, without all your stories and excuses, your past and your mishaps. So while you are doing this work, imagine that I am sitting with you. My clients always say they think of me offering them a safe space, encouraging ear and kick up the proverbial when it's needed. I aim to be that mirror for you, and the voice that will sit on your shoulder nudging you on.

A huge part of this journey into yourself is about trust – mostly trust in yourself, but also trust in me and what I will ask of you. While I never want you to do anything that feels out of alignment with who you are, I absolutely need you to be willing to go beyond your comfort zone and face aspects of yourself that you may not be comfortable with. I have interspersed the sometimes challenging exercises with inspirational stories from clients – real people like you who were brave enough to follow this journey.

When you're being stretched, rather than contracting into your default mode (probably the very glitch you may need to ditch) please reach out to me or to the community I have put in place to support you. There is no point in staying small and letting it all get the better of you. Unless, of course, that it is still serving you. We'll talk about that in the following pages.

Be daring. Be bold. No matter how scary, irritating or tiring it may be, it is worth it. Rise up, and be counted. It is your time!

Let's go!

MY PERSONAL GLITCH

Before we go any further, I have to admit that am not proud of everything I have done in my life, and yet at the same time, I can now say that I am proud of how I eventually handled it. I have made peace with parts of myself that I once judged and the things I have done that felt bad.

Are you proud of your life? Or is this why you want to embark on the journey within yourself, to make friends with yourself and to even start loving yourself? Have you made right the things you think were wrong, have you stood up for yourself and others, have you forgiven and let go, and are you reaching for your stars?

Perhaps you are currently somewhere in between?

There is something I am not particularly proud of. At the time I knew no other way of being with myself. In my late teen and early adult years, I was bulimic. Every day. For years.

I cannot remember how or where or when it started. (Of course, if I really wanted to I could go down the rabbit hole to find it, but I see no point anymore. It's done.)

Bulimia was a big personal glitch for a long time, one that I bore in silence. When I look back at pictures of myself at that time, I can see the mask I was wearing, and the pain hidden under the mask. My body was puffy and I was pretty overweight. I hardly even recognize myself. I don't know how many people knew what I was hiding at the time.

I grew up in a family of six, and as a kid I was teased for being fat. My dad called me "porky" and others named me "the Michelin Man". I was teased for having rolls of fat on my thighs. I knew that the teasing was affectionate, but it was also cruel and affected my body image.

My family would often gather in the kitchen a couple of hours after dinner, for delicious roast beef sandwiches and fresh onions bathed in vinegar, to have a catch up while scoffing. Then we'd all go our separate ways with a cup of tea, maybe a brandy for my dad, to contemplate life on the veranda, watch TV, read or study. I then developed the condition of "sleep eating". I would wake up in the morning and the only reason I knew I'd raided the kitchen was that I would find evidence in bed with me. I wasn't so worried about the men I'd find in my bed, but the food! Sometimes it was a piece of cheese on my cheek, a crust of toast under my shoulder or bacon on my pillow. Or I would eat something Mum was saving for the next day and then find that it was no longer in the fridge. Or I would come home from clubbing in standard nine, having drunk far too much with my boyfriend, and need food to soak up the booze. I'd blitz bacon in the microwave, so that the fat oozed on the plate, then slather that on white bread and smother it in cheese. I know that gloop solidified in my stomach within about two minutes. Then I would go to bed for a few hours before getting up to study. Great body nourishment.

There was another layer lurking underneath my sleep eating. It shifted to eating as much as possible, as secretly as possible, and then throwing up within about 20 minutes. I knew which foods would come back up easily. If I left it too long it became too acid, too sharp in my mouth. There was a sweet-spot time between eating and regurgitating, so I would plot and plan what to eat and when. When you are bulimic everything becomes about deception and sneaking off to the toilet as soon as you can. It's disgusting that I hated myself and my body so much as to put my finger down my throat. I got so good at it that, with one jerk of my index finger, I could regurgitate everything in my stomach. Then there was the routine of washing my face and hands, brushing my teeth, spraying on perfume and applying mascara, as tears would inevitably have streamed down my face from throwing up. Then it was back to normal. I once vomited up an entire chocolate cake!

NEVER GOOD ENOUGH

As a teenager, I used to drink quite a lot and party at varsity. I'd go clubbing every weekend, drive home and not remember doing it, sleep with too many boys and have too many one-night stands after I had my heart broken just a few times too many. It was regular teenage stuff that then translated into bulimia.

I think that externally I appeared to be a normal, regular person. I found it generally easy to make friends, flirt, and make good tips at Legends, a well-known restaurant in Musgrave. But there was always this self-loathing going on underneath, coupled with biting my nails, another sign of what was going on inside me.

Some memories still make me shudder if I allow myself to go there. Growing up, I was the youngest (and of course I still am) and it felt to me that more was expected from me than my brothers. I was expected to come first in class, get the best grades, be head girl, study something fabulous, and make bucketloads of money. But I never felt good enough. It's a bit of a family joke, but I could come home with 92%, the highest mark in my class, and my dad would say "so where's the other 8%?"

It was never good enough. I never felt good enough. Sometimes I would push myself to achieve, and sometimes my rebellious side would emerge and I'd let myself slip to a B average in high school.

I had an amazing childhood, but at a "poor me" level we all interpret everyday events in specific ways, because our needs are not met in the way we want them to be. We set up our glitch in response to our world. My parents, siblings and family never set out to mess with me intentionally. Neither did yours or anyone else's. We are all doing the best we can. And sometimes my best was to fill my face with food, then vomit it up again.

I was the only one in my family that "moved" around our home. I lived in four of the spaces available in my family home. My gypsy energy loved the newness of changing bedrooms. I loved it when I was in high school and went from upstairs, on the same floor as my parents, to the "outhouse". I was across a courtyard and separate from the main house. I had freedom!

I didn't have a bathroom and toilet in my bedroom, but I had a basin. I would be sick into it and then flood copious amounts of running water down the sink to wash it away. One day I realized that I had blocked the drain outside my room. I can still see it clearly now: The drain was painted matt black and there was a big heavy piece of concrete covering it. As I shifted the concrete to the side, to my horror, I found the entire thing blocked with ME, my built-up curdling vomit, my disgusting habit and self-loathing. I felt so embarrassed and paralyzed. I waited till night-time to try to unblock it, cleaning it out and putting drain cleaner down it. I couldn't believe my luck that no one had found it. Or had they just not said anything?

Of course that didn't stop me.

THE FINAL MOMENT

A couple of years later, after I completed varsity, I was working in a hotel in Gloucestershire. There was a lovely woman from the local village who cleaned and ironed for the hotel, and she looked after me like a daughter. One afternoon I happened to be out, so she decided to do something lovely and clean my room for me. When I came home she mentioned she'd changed my duvet and sheets, and vacuumed, but she wanted to know what was in my bin. I shrank back, knowing what she had found.

When I worked in the hotel, I used to go down to the kitchen at night – oh, imagine a walk-in fridge filled with goodies and delights and cakes and turkey curry and… What more could a night-time eater and bulimic girl ask for? I'd go down after midnight in my slippers and devour stuff for half an hour, standing in the fridge. And then grab crisps, pork scratchings and peanuts from the bar on my way back to my room. Thankfully I was allowed to eat what I wanted in the hotel, so I knew at least that I wasn't stealing. Just stealing from myself.

In my room, I used to throw up into a plastic shopping packet, and then find a time to dispose of it later in a toilet, as several staff members shared the same bathroom facilities. On this particular day, I had left a gold colored shopping packet, tied with a knot, filled with about three quarts of vomit in my bin. The woman had picked it up and wondered what on earth it was. I mumbled some answer, making up a fib, before running up to my room, horrified, mortified, embarrassed and ashamed. I think that was the final wake-up call. For the first time I felt someone had found me out and it was enough to jolt me into action.

JOURNEY TO SELF-ACCEPTANCE

Shortly afterwards I started traveling and went on the most memorable trip of my life. At just 22 I went to Southeast Asia for three months. I backpacked on my own in a totally foreign world.

When I got off the plane in Kathmandu, the first thing I saw was a dead cow being carved up on the side of the road, in 40 degree heat, flies buzzing in its insides, meat displayed everywhere. I decided I needed to have my wits about me. I knew I needed to look after myself as I was traveling alone. I became mindful of what I ate, stopped eating meat immediately, and started eating chilli, something I had never managed to do up until then.

It was a deeply spiritual journey for me and I started finding new ways to be with myself, to appreciate myself, to look after myself. I think it was when my real journey of self-acceptance started. I started to eat more healthily, drank very little and started losing weight naturally.

I feel very blessed that the rest of me never got sick (pardon the pun) as a direct result of bulimia. I know my body and mind suffer some small and manageable remnants from that time.

One of the results is that the very first thing I do when I wake up in the morning – before stroking my beloved cat, Stripey, or greeting a lover – is to place my right hand on my stomach and feel that part of my body. It's now a dialogue I have with myself. It's about saying hello, feeling how I'm doing, checking in that I'm looking after what I eat and drink, feeling whether I'm having a fat or thin day, telling me to get my butt out of bed to go to yoga. I can wake up feeling like I live in a different body to the one from the day before.

When I look back at my body journey, I used to go from fat to thin to fat phases, which was partnered with my bad relationships, being dumped by boyfriends for other women, feeling unloved and being madly in love with a man I wanted to marry who didn't feel the same way about me. Very little about me and my body was ever to do with my relationship with myself. It always seemed to be a reaction to everyone else.

More than a decade later a friend in London introduced me to Bikram yoga. I had practiced yoga on my own from books, but had never gone to classes. I was hooked from the first class and in one week could see and feel my body and soul transform. I felt sick every day from the sheer detoxification. It was a deeply intense process, but I knew I had found a perfectly balanced exercise for me.

The following year I found myself in Johannesburg, opening my life-coaching business at the same time that the first Bikram yoga studio opened in South Africa. I still practice there to this day, 12 years later, when I'm in Johannesburg.

Yoga is still my exercise of choice, for the profound insights I get from every class. Having yoga in my life in a regular way has been my biggest healing journey, one back to self-love, energy, and being more accepting of me and my body – loving it from a place of compassion so that it can be strong again. It took me a long time to learn to love my body. Outwardly it appeared that I did, but inwardly I was full of self-loathing. Our journey to healing and accepting our glitches is profound.

My biggest glitch was lack of self-worth, which then progressed to being too pushy in life. We will get to that in Step 4. I now constantly have to balance these glitches. My default is to just push harder and harder, to work too hard for too little in return. I'm learning the art of giving and receiving. The past 12 years of being a professional life coach have been an interesting journey. What I share and offer to you in the following pages are things that have worked for me and for my thousands of clients. It has taken me deeper into self-introspection.

WHEN THE RABBITS STOMP

I had another life-changing session that needed to unfold. I call it when the rabbits stomp.

When my personal rabbits came a-stomping, they started in a surreptitious way, until they stomped on my head one too many times and I was forced to face them at last. I am talking about depression and hormonal changes. And guys, don't think you are immune to this. I have a friend, who is South Africa's foremost fertility specialist – a homeopath who has "co-created" over 4 000 babies – and his specialty is the male and female hormonal cycle. He says every single one of us, old and young, male and female, is subject to the chemicals and hormones in our bodies.

I think because of my years of bulimic abuse, it took me a long time to even realize what was happening. I was on the verge of having uncontrollable mood swings. The rabbit that made me wake up was my demanding little Bengal cat, Benu. He looked at up at me one too many times, meowing incessantly, and my world came tumbling down around me. It's strange just how infinitesimally small that last straw can be. All Benu really wanted was a little fish treat and another ear tickle, but it was my undoing. I had a million self-created chores, tasks, expectations and a constant supply of bloody bunnies I had been pulling out of the hat, and it all just got too much. I reached the moment where I literally screamed, "ENOUGH!" What a great place to get to: the rabbits had kicked harder and harder until I was finally forced to pay attention.

The morning after I collapsed on the floor in tears, with my kitty weaving through my legs, I met a dear friend for coffee around the corner from where I was seeing clients. I had managed to pull myself together for my first client, then dashed to visit my friend. I have always described myself as energetic, feisty, enthusiastic and even irritatingly positive to people, like a Duracell bunny on happy juice. Even while battling bulimia, my external life appeared superb. I have always appreciated my ability to find solutions and be creative. My entire life has been about that. That morning as I sat down with my friend, I thought we were about to talk about her. But she simply asked me, "How are you doing, Kate?"

You know that moment when someone who loves you asks you that question sincerely and your whole soul responds? I was sitting opposite her with big watery eyes and then shoulder-hunching sobs. What was worse was that I knew I had to be ready in two hours for my second client, and mascara dripping down my face was not exactly high on my "client-appropriate appearance" list.

In that moment, having to answer my friend's question, is where my idea of the "stomping rabbits" came from. What I blurted out as I sobbed and spluttered into my coffee, was that I had been a rabbit-pulling magician all my life, and yet at that moment I was sitting at the bottom of the damn magician's hat, with all the rabbits I had ever pulled out into the world stomping on my head. I was in utter agony. They were in control, and I had no power.

At the same time, I could not tell her why I was being stomped on. I was doing my life's work, with a full life coaching practice that was flourishing; I was in an interesting and ever-deepening relationship; I was doing better financially than I had ever done in my life; I was meeting amazing business connections; I was living the life I wanted and envisioned. And yet I was a complete misery. I kept saying to her I didn't know what was wrong or what to do. I felt pathetic, useless, a failure – you name it. I also felt like a fraud. How could I say I was loving what I was doing and be a crying pathetic loser?

But this is the interesting bit: the very next day I was my old, happy rabbit-pulling self. A week or three later, the rabbits were stomping again. A couple of days later the magician re-appeared. It was exhausting. A rollercoaster ride of hell. The funny thing was that when I was being the magician, I forgot I was ever stomped on. All memory of it was obliterated. Luckily it never really affected my work, but it was affecting my ability to be me.

It took the observations of other people in my life to help me realize that the rabbits were actually stomping on my head quite systematically and regularly. About once a month. The penny dropped. I was starting to finally think about the concept that I was suffering from hormonally induced imbalances and depression – something entirely foreign to me, superwoman! Once I realized that this depression could be related to my cycle and my hormones, I could do something about it. But I was still stubborn.

For me the journey initially was quite simple: supplements, flower essences, meditation, homeopathic medicine, more exercise. This meant that every now and then a cute little bunny would tickle my head for a fleeting moment, but no more huge rabbits with big feet. But I never completely got the better of it, and I slowly started slacking off on the things I was doing to stay healthy.

Externally everything seemed to be going well, but I was still a wreck inside. I guess once again I was hiding things from myself and the world.

COMING CLEAN

I had relocated to Cape Town with my partner, and was traveling back and forth to Johannesburg to service my coaching clients. It felt amazing. Then the 2008 recession hit. Most of my clients were self-employed or owned small businesses, and 2008 was a really tough year in South Africa. We had load shedding, petrol went up umpteen times, and everyone was tightening his or her belt. I let go of some important aspects of my business, like client service. I think I stopped caring for a while as I just didn't have the energy. My partner and I made some really ill-thought-through financial decisions together and individually, as we got into extreme financial stress on every front. I was getting more and more depressed because I had stopped working as much, and with the recession I didn't travel to Johannesburg as often. There were many, many days when I had to choose between buying pre-paid electricity, petrol, milk, or food for our six animals. We were living a lifestyle that looked rosy on the outside, yet was vacant and depressed on the inside.

I eventually fell into an even bigger hat with larger rabbits. Warrens of them. I had taken an internal issue and made it external. I was messing with my life, my finances, my home and my partnership. It got the point where I had not billed for any work for three months, all my payments were in arrears, and I was about to lose my Johannesburg property that I rented out. There were times when I even felt suicidal. That's how shitty it all was. And yet I was still trying to wear the mask, get clients, be the effervescent life coach.

I cried every day. Nothing made sense. I was clearly not on top of my depression and because I was feeling depressed, I was not manifesting work, and that created more stress, which added to my depression. I was also feeling like a total fraud. How on earth was I meant to help anyone if I was not coping with life myself? It got so bad that I finally had to come clean and tell my family the truth. I had to have the two hardest and most courageous conversations in my life. My mom was coming out from the UK for her 70th birthday bash and us kids were all clubbing together to buy her a bespoke gift by an artist in Stellenbosch; plus we were all going on a five-star holiday. I had to phone her and say I was not going to be able to go away; I was hardly able to put food on our table. That single act of calling and being completely honest was a total relief. Coming clean was the real turning point for me. Then I called my younger brother, whom I am very close to. I had to start off typing on Skype, with tears falling on my keyboard, telling him just how dire things had gotten for me and that I was pulling the plug on the holiday and the present. I wrote, "I have made such a mess of things and I'm in real trouble." He made it instantly better when he typed back: "Why, did you kill someone?" I was able to heave a sigh of relief knowing it wasn't that bad for me; it was immediate perspective.

I felt like such a failure though, as everyone had thought I was doing so well with my new business. No one knew that I was hiding and that I was in the throes of losing everything. The moment I started asking for help was when little miracles started happening. It still took another two months until I made another courageous call, this time to a former boss in Johannesburg, and asked for some work in the restaurant industry. His response to me was, "How soon can you get here?" I knew it was going to be all right.

I had to finally grow up and face reality. The next courageous conversation was with my partner to say that the work I could get was in Johannesburg and I needed a change of scenery. To be honest, we needed a change of scenery from each other too. My life was telling me I was on the wrong path with the wrong person, and I needed to get back to me. I had to drive away from my home by the sea, five of my six animals, my Harley Davidson, and my morning walks on the beach: my entire life in Cape Town. But I had to do it to survive.

I was very blessed to have unbelievable support from my partner's family (until we split up), my mum, and my younger brother and his partner, who let me live in their home and didn't mind me coming home at 4 a.m. after my restaurant shift ended. It was a couple of months before I could even contribute to paying for food, let alone pay them back the money they had lent me. I was working about 80 hours a week in a gorgeous three-storey restaurant, night club and cocktail lounge. I remember the joy I felt as I cried because my feet and body were sore from hard work, rather than from stress and depression.

THE TALE OF TWO CASINOS

I kept repeating to myself, "If I can get through this moment, this hour, this time, I can get through anything." Personally, I have never been one for the weird energy of casinos, but this just happened to be where my job was, and so six days a week, I would drive from Melville to Krugersdorp and work insane hours. It even got to the point where I would sleep on the casino couches after a Saturday night shift as I had to open up at 9 a.m. on a Sunday, and the 30-minute trek to and from home just didn't seem worth the sleep time. I once wrote a blog post about how many pairs of shoes I broke that year – seven! That's how hard I worked. And I got my life back.

It turned out to be the most amazing year of my life, but in retrospect, that I need not have put myself, my partner, businesses, lifestyle, friends and family through all the stress. I was seriously stubborn in terms of not listening to what my rabbits were trying to get through to me! Leaving behind that so-called ideal life I had created, and everything that no longer served me or my higher purpose, gave me a new opportunity at life again. I started having fun, laughing, meeting people and finding myself again. That year was a defining one for me.

I decided for that year to just keep a log of wood on the fire that was my life-coaching business. I kept writing newsletters and would take on clients for coaching if they found me. I knew I was just taking a breather and that I would get back to my purpose soon enough. That was 2009. Later that year I was the recipient of a Feather Award for my contribution to transforming women's lives in South Africa and it gave me hope and inspiration that I would one day come back to this path of helping others. In the meantime I kicked ass in the hospitality industry and had a ball.

It is now six years later. In yoga class on the morning that I wrote this introduction, I was struck by the irony of the trip to America that I was preparing for, to be part of a self-development movie in Las Vegas. The producer asked all the experts to book into the same hotel. In yoga I started giggling inwardly when I realized I was going back to yet another casino! I had a moment of being totally in awe of the interwoven circle of life, and I got teary writing this. We can't always know everything that is to come in our life; we can only follow our intuition and our heart when we are able to. Otherwise life will kick us there. I feel humbled when I witness the last six-year cycle of my own personal journey of growth. I feel as if I have lived and learned more in the last six years than the rest of my life. It is a time of immense stepping up, after having let go of everything I once believed in. That turning point of coming clean with my family and leaving my life in Cape Town defined the next phase of my life. I now travel the world doing what I love, and live a life of authenticity.

YOU CAN TOO!

Be brave, my beautiful reader.

Every time I have personally been able to make significant shifts, either to up the ante, move through the pain of limiting beliefs, or let go of a heartache, it was because I could own up to the part of me that was being served by my glitch.

Every time I let someone else's opinion matter more than my own, I was soothing the part of me that didn't believe I was good enough. Every time I accepted less money than my services were worth, it fed the monster that told me I didn't deserve money, that I was meant to struggle. Every time I accepted less than because I felt less than, it entrenched the belief that I was truly less than. When you know it is time to ditch your glitch, you have to put on your big girl panties, or your Superman undies, and deal with it head on.

I shared some snippets of my life in these pages for a few reasons. It is self-healing at the most selfish (self-full!) of levels, because by sharing our stories we heal our past and help others to do the same. I believe that when we share, we give other people permission to own their stories so they can transform them. Also, I hope to inspire you to live a more profound and engaged life by coming to terms with every aspect of who you are.

I have used many tools on my journey. I urge you to try out everything I offer in this book, just once, and then at the end decide which exercises really work for you. Those are the ones to keep. Make your introspective journey your own, dear friend.

Accept who you are right now.

Take my hand on this journey: your life is waiting!

I love you as I love myself.

With compassion, wisdom from insight, a huge sense of humor and kick up the butt when needed,

Kate

AUTOBIOGRAPHY IN FIVE SHORT CHAPTERS

CHAPTER ONE:
I walk down the street.
There is a deep hole in the sidewalk.
I fall in.
I am lost… I am hopeless.
It isn't my fault.
It takes forever to find a way out.

CHAPTER TWO:
I walk down the same street.
There is a deep hole in the sidewalk.
I pretend I don't see it.
I fall in again.
I can't believe I'm in this same place.
But it isn't my fault.
It still takes a long time to get out.

CHAPTER THREE:
I walk down the same street.
There is a deep hole in the sidewalk.
I see it is there.
I still fall in… it's a habit… but,
My eyes are open.
I know where I am.
I am lost… I am hopeless.
It is my fault.
I get out immediately.

CHAPTER FOUR:
I walk down the same street.
There is a deep hole in the sidewalk.
I walk around it.

CHAPTER FIVE:
I walk down another street.

Portia Nelson, *There's a Hole in My Sidewalk:*
The Romance of Self-Discovery (Beyond Words Publishing, 1994)

The process

"Our duty is wakefulness, the fundamental condition of life itself. The unseen, the unheard, the untouchable is what weaves the fabric of our see-able universe together."
Robin Craig Clark, *The Garden*

What is going to unfold in this process ahead? Before we get stuck into your life, let's get an overview of what we're going to do.

PART 1: STEPPING IN
You will start off by honestly assessing and taking stock of your life as it is now. This is one of my favourite exercises as it's simple, yet offers profound insights into eight areas of your life.

You will also be asking significant people in your life for feedback on certain things. That might feel pretty scary to you right now, but gaining insight is invaluable to evaluating who we are.

We are often not consciously aware of the stories that we weave and so we keep going back to the same glitches over and over again. Those who truly love and respect us, who have wisdom and insight, are an invaluable source of information. We need to be willing to listen and receive their wisdom.

Part of this process is understanding the five most common glitches, so you can figure out what has been holding you back. By identifying with the mechanism that might be sabotaging you, you can start to unpack it, re-wire it and ditch it. This step requires courage, hope, inspiration and a whole lot of guts.

PART 2: STEPPING UP
When you successfully understand your glitch and you are honest about where you are starting this work from – your life today – then you are able to ignite your life. This concept revolves around how each of us holds an eternal flame inside our heart. Every now and then things get out of control and we feel like we are at the bottom of the heap. It can feel as though the flame in our soul has gone out, like a bucket of cold water has been tossed on our fire and killed it.

The practical tools in this section provide the "how to" for shifting your life. You'll learn to ask for more, expect more, and believe you deserve more. This centres on deciding what you want in all eight areas of life and taking the steps to work towards what you deserve, while ditching that which no longer serves you.

> **PART 3: STEPPING OUT**
>
> Stepping out is about taking your newly ignited life, now that you have let go of all the sabotaging ideas, patterns and glitches, and sharing your real self with the world.
>
> How do you shine your light in a profoundly authentic way? Where to from here? How do you keep going when the going gets tough? (And it will get tough.) How do you not let life pull you off track again, or more importantly, how do you get back on track faster when you get derailed?
>
> In this part of the process, we'll cover how you can keep shining your light, even when it feels like it might be easier to fall back into old habits.

COMMITMENT

> *"If you change the way you look at things, the things you look at change."*
> Dr Wayne Dyer

Commitment is needed from you to complete the exercises in this book. I will ask you to:
- Sign a commitment form.
- Carve out time every day to do this work.
- Engage with the support community.

Please take a few deep breaths, gird your loins, read the following commitment form and sign it. Just as with any legal contract, take some time to read it all. This act alone could bring up all sorts of stories in your mind and excuses about why you shouldn't do it – all making you feel a little nervous. It's okay!

Take a photo of this commitment form and use it as the screen saver on your phone.

COMMITMENT TO ME, MYSELF AND I

I, ...,
am ready and willing to give everything required to DITCH MY GLITCH so that I can IGNITE MY LIFE again. I am ready to achieve my goals and expand my life by actively participating in everything in this book. This will require time and dedication from me.

No matter how many buttons they might push, I will do my utmost to do all the exercises put before me by Kate. I will also activate a support network of people who wholeheartedly support my growth, no matter what.

I will be gentle yet firm as I embark on this journey of shifting my life. It matters not where I've come from; what matters more is how I choose to face up to myself now and how willing I am to be honest about the life I really want.

I acknowledge that I am responsible for what happens in my life and the choices I have made, which also means I will find the strength to make the necessary changes to live an awesome life.

So be it.

Name: .... Date: ....

Signed: ....

"Until one is committed there is hesitancy, the chance to draw back, always ineffectiveness. Concerning all acts of initiative (and creation), there is one elementary truth that ignorance of which kills countless ideas and splendid plans, that the moment one definitely commits oneself, then Providence moves too. All sorts of things occur to help one that would never otherwise have occurred. A whole stream of events issues from the decision, raising in one's favor all manner of unforeseen incidents and meetings and material assistance, which no man could have dreamed would have come his way. Whatever you can do, or dream you can do, begin it. Boldness has genius, power and magic in it. Begin it now."
William Hutchinson Murray

Time out

What is required to ditch your glitch so that you can ignite your life is to spend at least an hour a day on your life so that you can get the benefits and outcomes you really want. This is about managing your time and energy.

And yes, I mean an hour a day! I know it is tempting to want a break from it all on the weekend, but habits take between 25 and 30 days to create, and so you need to put in the time consistently to reap the rewards.

How are you going to give this to yourself?

- You may need to schedule "appointments" with yourself in your diary. It will not happen if you let each day unfold haphazardly. If you have a "date" with yourself every day, you will soon start noticing if you are or aren't getting around to it when you vigilantly re-assess your day every evening.
- You may need to extricate yourself from certain obligations that you have taken on.
- You may need to learn to say no. Oh boy, that's a hard one, hey?
- You may need to get up earlier or go to sleep later.
- You may need to eat and hydrate yourself differently to keep your energy levels up.
- You might need to have conversations with the key people in your life to get the support you need.
- Most of all, you will need creativity and commitment as you carve out time to pay attention to your life every single day.

No one else can do this for you, and perhaps right now the hesitancy to make time for yourself is in fact the biggest glitch you need to face. Do what you need to do now to carve out time and put yourself back on your own priority list.

Join the community for support

I've created a private Facebook group where you can share your inspirational stories and challenges on your journey. You'll be supported and encouraged by me and others who are doing this work. You will also receive all the worksheets in the book.

This is a closed group and is only for clients who are working through my courses and books. There is no charge to participate, and it is my way of giving you additional nudges and support along the way.

To join, send an email to shift@kate-emmerson.com with "REQUEST TO JOIN DITCH YOUR GLITCH" in the subject line.

There are plenty of other ways you can stay in touch with me:

- Facebook: www.facebook.com/kate-emmerson.page
- Website: www.kate-emmerson.com
- Twitter: @kate_emmerson
- LinkedIn: www.linkedin.com/in/kateemmerson

CLIENT INSPIRATION

The Ignite Your Life course stirred things up for me. I dealt with things that had been smoldering for ages and baggage that I'd been dragging around for years.

Right through the process Kate and others in the group were a constant support. The fabulous check-in system allowed for constant support every step of the way. Being able to share and connect with others (a lot of the time we were experiencing the same feelings and thoughts) made the journey shine.

At the time the song *Firework* by Katy Perry was a hit and it captures the essence of this course. It lights me up inside every time I hear it. A fabulous reminder.

> You just gotta
> Ignite the light
> And let it shine
> Just own the night
> Like the fourth of July
>
> 'Cause baby, you're a firework
> Come on show them what you're worth
> Make them go, "Oh, oh, oh"
> As you shoot across the sky
>
> ...
> Like a lightning bolt
> Your heart will glow

I highly recommend this to everyone.
M, Johannesburg

YOUR TOOLKIT

Having the right tools from the start will make your journey of self-discovery easier and more fun, and will save you time along the way.

Here's a list of what you need to gather before you get stuck into step one.

A beautiful journal

Take yourself on a "date" to your favorite bookstore or stationers and allow yourself to wander through the journal section and pick something that entices you to write in it. The inside pages could be plain, lined or colored, the cover could be soft or hard, dark or bright. I love to choose a cover that embodies the work I'm about to embark on. Imagine choosing a journal that actually twinkles at you from your desk, begging you to inscribe its pages.

While you are there, why not buy yourself a beautiful pen, one that feels comfortable and energetic in your hands. It may seem simple but I have often found that having a beautiful journal with a specific pen supports and encourages me to go within. Why not try it?

"One advantage in keeping a diary is that you become aware with reassuring clarity of the changes which you constantly suffer and which in a general way are naturally believed, surmised, and admitted by you, but which you'll unconsciously deny when it comes to the point of gaining hope or peace from such an admission. In the diary you find proof that in situations which today would seem unbearable, you lived, looked around and wrote down observations, that this right hand moved then as it does today, when we may be wiser because we are able to look back upon our former condition, and for that very reason have got to admit the courage of our earlier striving in which we persisted even in sheer ignorance."
Franz Kafka, from *Diaries of Franz Kafka*

A gorgeous candle

If you are inspired by fragranced candles, buy one that will help you feel aligned to your journey. For example, there are certain fragrances that I find soothing, nourishing and spiritually uplifting, such as geranium, neroli, frankincense and rose. These are my personal choices for accompanying *Ditch Your Glitch*. To focus and clarify your thoughts, you might want to try mint, rosemary, grapefruit or lemon grass.

Whether you choose a fragranced or plain candle, ensure that it is a color you resonate with, and is big enough to burn for at least 48 hours.

A vision board

You will start thinking like a kid again as you make this, so we're talking about the following: an A1 piece of cardboard, crayons, glitter, glue, scissors, stickers and at least 10 of your favorite magazines. As you will see when we get to the exercise, you may want different kinds of magazines, such as travel, spirituality, health, finances, and anything else that inspires you to be the best version of yourself.

"Everything you want is just outside your comfort zone."
Robert Allen

YOUR DAILY RITUAL

"The secret of getting ahead is getting started."
Mark Twain

I asked you to gather a few things for your toolkit as you embark on your journey – your beautiful candle and journal are part of your daily ritual. Here's why…

Ignite your personal flame

Every day when you spend your hour on your life, you will first light your candle as a reminder that you are doing everything you can to ignite your personal flame. Let your candle burn while you find your own fire. It is a beautiful intentional way to keep you focused and on fire every day.

Gratitude journaling

You will be writing in your journal every day. I am going to challenge you to write a gratitude journal in which you note all the amazing things that you are already grateful for in your life.

Even if you feel as though your fire is totally dead and your life is being ruled by your personal glitch-ometer, one of the best exercises is to be mindful of what exists already.

I suggest you AIM for 12 small things every day; they can be anything you choose. Do not simply repeat the same list every day, but rather wander back through the last 24 hours and find the things that you are truly grateful for. Why am I asking you to do this?

One of the principles that you can start working with is that like attracts like. I am not planning to get too airy-fairy on you but this is one of the principles offered up by the universe. If you are spending all day moaning and bitching about how bad stuff is, well then, hey presto, there you have it. Have you ever noticed the people who speak badly about their lives are the ones who have a "badly designed" life? And the ones who speak highly of their life, with mindfulness and consciousness, have better, happier and more fulfilled lives?

How would you currently identify yourself? Do you live with gratitude or show up with a bad-itude?

Gratitude	Bad-itude
More conscious	Unconscious robot
Trusting	Disbelieving
Accepting	Resisting
Flowing	Constricted
Energized	Stagnant
Calm	Stressed
Pro-active	Reactive
Engaged	Disinterested
Creative	Blocked
Willing	Closed off
Victor	Victim

I find that when I am feeling down in the dumps or mad at the world, the quickest way to shift stuff externally, and correspondingly shift myself internally, is to focus on different things, no matter how hard it might be. I might also simply want to kick and scream, and sometimes I will give my inner-brat permission to do just that, but with a cut-off period. Then I come back to gratitude.

When you are feeling as if your fire is out and you have no energy, that your glitches are running or ruining your life, it can seem impossible to find any magic, have fun, be creative and do anything other than simply dragging your heels through your day. But what happens is that your entire being, mentally, emotionally, spiritually and even physically, starts resonating to that specific feeling: the feeling of being down.

It's like you
… have no life.
… are in crisis mode.
… always have to rush.
… are out of control.
… can't make anything work.
… are always stressed.
… and on and on it goes.

It creates a downward spiral, with you at the bottom of that horrid hole. If there is something that you want more of in your life, the place to start is by acknowledging what is already working in an awesome and positive way, no matter how minuscule it is to begin with.

I know that it might seem easy to say, "Yes Kate, but when things get better I will feel better and then I will start writing positive things." I am here to share with you that it is of benefit to start paying attention to the good right now, even amidst the chaos. This is what will help you see your glitches and ignite your fire. It is fine if you don't believe me right now, but I am challenging you to do it anyway, and the proof will be in the experience.

Because like attracts like, I promise that very soon you will start noticing more of what is right, and less of what is wrong. Perception is everything. When you are in crisis, ruled by your glitches and your fire feels non-existent, that is all you are allowing yourself to see. When you start acknowledging the presence of something else, it is like the matches have been found, and the flame can be re-lit. So AIM to write 12 things that you are grateful for in your life every day.

TIP: I am part of a group that we call the DDs – Daily Dozen. To be honest, we do not all email each other every day, but we do so a few times a week. I used to do gratitude journaling on my own, but have found this more powerful because someone else gets to witness my musings and I also get to witness other people being grateful in their lives, which nudges me to do the same. The power of group energy is tenfold, so use it to your benefit whenever you can. Nowadays, I do a combination of writing my DDs for myself, mailing my group, along with saying aloud what I am grateful for when I'm driving.

> *"What you think about, talk about and get off your ass and do something about, comes about."*
> Larry Winget

"It may sound odd, but the fastest way to get a new and improved situation is to make peace with your current situation. By making lists of the most positive aspects you can find about your current situation, you then release your resistance to improvements that are waiting for you. But if you rail against the injustices of your current situation, you hold yourself in vibrational alignment with that which you do not want, and you cannot then move in the direction of improvement. It defies law. In every particle of the universe there is that which is wanted, and the lack of it."
Abraham Hicks

My story

Four years ago I was spending a much needed rest-and-rejuvenation weekend in the area known as Nottingham Road in KwaZulu-Natal with my partner. We were booked into a beautiful cottage that backed up onto a spectacular indigenous forest. It was beyond wow! The first morning we explored the old trees, ferns, sculptures and pathways that stretched up the hill behind the cottage.

I had recently started a walking program, but let's be honest – I was by no means fit, fabulous or with great lung capacity. Yet I found myself on this beautiful pathway stretching enticingly up the hill before me. It was bad enough that I had to by-pass the gnarled roots stretched across the dirt pathway, avoid low-hanging branches, look for spider webs and keep my stomach in (something I had been taught about running was to activate your core at all times) – but I really, really wanted the kick of having gotten up that darn hill. I didn't know where to look – up at the endpoint or down at my feet.

Spontaneously, from somewhere deep inside me, I started chanting (while gasping):
If I choose to, then I want to.
If I want to, then I can.
If I can, then I must.
If I must, then I will!

I kept repeating it like a mantra or prayer, over and over again. I am filled with gratitude for it as it gave me the concept of choice. It gave me a burst of energy, a flash of inspiration and much-needed power to get up that hill, which seemed to go on forever. That saying has since become one of my life mottos. When I'm attempting to stretch myself emotionally or physically, for example standing on one leg in Bikram yoga, but I feel a little wobbly and unstable, I do my best and start repeating this.

Do you have a motto, saying, prayer or mantra that keeps you on track and in touch with yourself, urging you on no matter what?

Let's get back to your daily ritual. The third aspect is fire rating.

"Fire-rating" journaling

It's a bit early to set your journal on fire! When you have found the (12) things that you are grateful for, this is the next step.

Ask yourself every day, "How do I rate my 'personal fire energy' today?" on a scale of one to 10, with 10 being absolutely awesome and the flame burning brightly, and one feeling like a damp squib.

Close your eyes and feel it – take some deep breaths and come to your heart center to find the flame in your heart and soul. It might feel really dim and small or even extinguished. No matter what, just get a sense of where it is right now. That flicker of flame is with you every moment of the day and night. Its potential sits there, no matter what.

You might need to find matches and gunpowder to ignite that little flame or throw wood, petrol and oxygen on it to keep it glowing.

All you have to do is notice it. The actual number you allocate it doesn't matter, just that you be honest each day. This number will obviously change according to how you feel on any given day.

Next ask yourself, "What one small thing can I do today that will increase my personal fire and shift it up, even if it's just a tiny bit?" You then respond to your gut, intuition or heart and find something that you are in control of, that you can take action on, that will help you to feel like you are fanning the flame of your heart fire. It is a simple yet profoundly powerful exercise, as it gives you a daily way to assess life and look at what you can immediately do to increase your fire.

It's the start of taking active responsibility every day. No more sitting around feeling sorry for yourself about what others are or aren't doing to you or for you. No one can make you feel better but you. This exercise alone can help you to take huge strides towards being in control. Have fun with it.

POINTS TO REMEMBER EVERY DAY
- Light your candle.
- Add 12 things to your gratitude list.
- Rate your fire energy on a scale of one to 10 and journal about how you can take action to immediately increase it.
- Then tackle the next challenge in the step-by-step process as you progress through this book.
- Breathe right now. Breathe into the possibility of all that can be in your life.

Part 1
Stepping in

> *"Character cannot be developed in ease and quiet. Only through experience of trial and suffering can the soul be strengthened, vision cleared, ambition inspired, and success achieved."*
> Helen Keller

"Come into my parlor said the spider to the fly," I remember my Nan saying when I was growing up, in a weird voice that used to make me squeal. We all know that the fly gets eaten by the hungry spider.

I often think that doing any form of inner work can be scary, daunting, overwhelming and plain intimidating. Like the fly walking into a trap, except that it's a trap we've made ourselves. We shy away from going inside and yet that means we never experience the joy of freedom that awaits us on the other side of the inner work. Allow that to pull you through the process. I believe that every time you shy away from the work, it will only become more entrenched and lodge itself in every cell of your body. I have learned that, and I'm sure you have too along your journey. Perhaps today is the day you have decided to make a new choice and take a new path forwards.

Your life is waiting for you to assess where you are, reignite your flame, take action and get back on track.

Everything that you have ever thought, experienced, felt, believed and done has gotten you to this point in your life. This means that if you are ready for something different, you will have to create new patterns, habits, beliefs and ways.

> *"If you always do what you have always done, then you will always get what you have always got."*
> Henry Ford

Read that again.

The equation is simple. Your past created today. Today creates tomorrow.

You have the power to make this moment matter by being present in it. If you do not like now, change it today so that tomorrow is in line with the *you* that you want to be. Everything we do over the course of this book will build around this simple concept.

STEP 1:
Take stock of your life

> *"There are two primary choices in life: to accept conditions as they exist or to accept responsibility for changing them."*
> Unknown

Make yourself something to drink and then get stuck into this great exercise. It's one of my favorites for assessing where you are right now.

My story

I first did this exercise in 2003 when I was studying life coaching, and I realized just how badly out of kilter my life was. I had just been to France to work as an executive chef in a very posh villa for two months. It sounds absolutely glamorous, and it was in the most beautiful part of Provence, yet it was back-breaking work. I spent 17 hours every day looking at lavender fields while I cooked breakfast, lunch, evening canapés and three-course dinners for 16 guests. The chefs also had to clean the kitchen, shop, plan menus and handle the guests' foibles and daily demands.

There is only one photo of me at work in that time, and I'm in the villa kitchen, totally blurred. That photo epitomizes the time I spent there, as I was in a whirlwind – never stopping to smell the lavender or the rosemary. Yet I would not have changed it for the world. How many non-chefs get to say they did that in their lives? The main point of doing the work was to earn pounds to fund my professional life-coaching course. To be honest, it was the most dosh a week I had earned at that point in my life. But I got to the UK totally exhausted and frazzled. I had also suspected my partner, who joined me in France for this work, was cheating on me – something that was confirmed when I dared to ask the question. (Sometimes we just don't want to ask the question, even when we know deep down what the answer is.)

At that time my mum was diagnosed with cervical cancer, a year to the day after my dad passed way from cancer, and I was going to stay with her while I studied coaching in the UK. The universe orchestrated it perfectly for me to be with my mum when she needed me and I needed her.

But, back to the cycle of life exercise. It was the very first exercise I did as part of the life-coaching course. Its simplicity just blew me away, and still does. I am pretty sure you might have come across it already, and chances are you might even say, "Oh, I know that exercise". It can be called the cycle of life, the circle of life, the wheel of life etc. You can take it seriously or pass it by, but in my experience, in my own life and with clients, it is one of the most powerful exercises and is filled with the most potential.

Doing the exercise, I realized that I was doing pretty shabbily in the fun and finance parts of my life. I had been putting so much attention on the next part of my career, and working my butt off to get the funds together, that I was stressed about finances and not having any fun whatsoever. My finances and fun were both sitting on about 10% and they were throwing everything else off balance. And you can imagine that my relationships were not faring much better after I found out about my partner's "betrayal". I realized I had been connecting needing money to having fun, and I was dependent on what my partner at the time wanted from me and what I believe I deserved. I was not taking time to rest or play, and this exercise made me understand that unless I started balancing my life, planning for holidays and time off, I was going to lose my sense of self. And more importantly, how on earth could I become a great coach if I wasn't taking all eight areas of myself into account? It truly opened my eyes, and I sincerely hope it does the same for you.

Warning! The four most dangerous words are, "Oh, I know that!"

Please put yourself on notice and start being vigilant about your words and thoughts. When you think or utter the words "Oh, I know that", it is like you are covering yourself in a big sheet of heavy metal, from top to bottom. It shuts you off from the world and not one ounce of inspiration will be able to break through that armor plating. You do yourself such a disservice by not allowing for the possibility of change and being open to a new experience this time around. So please notice when you are saying those four words.

CYCLE OF LIFE

The cycle of life is a great self-development tool. Go step by step and enjoy the process. There are eight sections, which depict your life, in the circle:

- health and fitness
- relationships and communication
- leisure and fun
- career
- spirituality
- self-development
- finances
- home and family

Let's chat a bit about these and what they mean.

Health and fitness

Health is such a pivotal aspect to the other seven areas. This is how we gather energy and fuel, which then sustains us to carry out the things we most want to do. It "feeds" all the other pieces of the pie.

This is about having more than "just sufficient" energy to drag yourself through the day. It is about having the physical "vooma" (oh, I love that word) to constructively and consistently act upon your goals. Do you find you have too much day at the end of your energy reserves, and prefer the idea of TV and sleeping rather than dancing, enjoying your hobby, spending time with your kids, or a romantic night out?

Relationships and communication
This is about your relationship with yourself, first and foremost. Do you like and trust yourself, put yourself on your own priority list, speak the truth, and feel in alignment with your life? Do you feel heard? Then, how do you interact with and communicate with others in your world, be they your partner, friends, colleagues or strangers?

Leisure and fun
How much time off do you give yourself to rest, recuperate, play, be with kids, do things that make you happy, laugh and sizzle? When we neglect this area of life, we become dull, boring, grumpy and resentful, often as a result of working too hard. Fun is an attitude to life, not necessarily about spending lots of money on exciting things. What floats your boat?

Career
This is the part of your life where you bring yourself, your talents, skills, experience, and education, and share them with the world. It doesn't matter whether you're employed, entrepreneurial, a stay-at-home mum or dad, or doing volunteer work. Do you feel like you are contributing in a way that is worthwhile and enables you to follow your passion?

Spirituality
This about your connection to something bigger than yourself. It can be religion, but it can also be about nature, spirit and a way of being in the world. When the going gets tough, do you have somewhere to turn, to give thanks and to ask for guidance and support? Do you feel connected to something intangible? Do you feel an overriding greater purpose for your life?

Self-development
This concept covers many things you do or want to do in your life. It is about how you choose to "up the ante", to step outside your comfort zone and challenge yourself. It's anything that will improve you directly or indirectly. I classify workshops, courses or study (if it doesn't pertain directly to your career) under this area. This is about learning something new. Do you feel as if you are growing?

Finances
Are you where you want to be with this piece of pie? Think of your salary or income, assets, will, retirement, being in control of your money, debt levels, how you feel about money, etc. If you have a family you are responsible for, have you considered what needs to be in place should you get ill, are unable to earn an income, or die? Do you have financial freedom?

Home and family

This area of life pertains to the people we are connected to genetically, and those we consider our "chosen" family. It's also about the physical space in which we eat, live and sleep. Is your life supported by this piece of pie? Are you energized when you walk into your home and does it feel safe, sacred and warm to you? Are your conversations with your family as you wish them to be?

HOW TO COMPLETE AND EVALUATE YOUR CYCLE OF LIFE

TIP: You can write in the book itself if that works for you, or you can simply re-draw the diagram in your journal.

See diagram 1 on page 146

Please follow the instructions as they appear, without jumping ahead to see what is required of you next.

The very center of the circle where all the lines meet represents 0%, or completely unsatisfied, with this area of your life right now. The current outer edge of the circle represents 100%, or totally satisfied with this area of your life right now.

Contemplate each section in turn. While every facet of our lives is intertwined with the next, when doing this exercise it's useful to compartmentalize them to begin with. Be really honest with yourself so that you can gain the most benefit from this.

Draw a line across each section to make a new outer edge in response to how you feel you are doing in this area right now. For example, if you feel that you are 50% satisfied with your career, draw a new edge halfway between the center point and the outer rim of the circle, in the career section. Use curved lines for the new outer perimeters so they mirror the circle edge.

See diagram 2 on page 147

Do this for each of the eight sections. It helps if you color in each of your newly drawn sections, from the center to the new line.

See diagram 3 on page 148

Please note: Evaluate each of the eight sections on their own out of 100%. The entire circle put together does not add up to 100%.

Great. Now look honestly at your diagram and answer the following:
1. What kind of circle have you got?
2. Look at the edge of your circle. Is it a perfect circle?
3. Imagine you are a bird flying over your own life. What one word or phrase best describes your current circle, i.e. your life? (Strong language is very common when first doing this exercise.)

4. Now look at the circle in a slightly different way. Can you see any interesting connections or interactions between any of the segments? For example, is one section of your life taking away valuable time or energy from another? Notice what is opposite each other, next to each other. What are your responses to this exercise? Take some time to sit with this and feel what it means for you and you alone.
5. Now take some quiet time to reflect deeply and write a detailed paragraph about each of the eight aspects of your life to explain why you have allotted it that particular percentage. What is causing it to be the way it is? What patterns are you aware of that might be keeping you stuck here?

Now that you have completed the cycle of life exercise, you will have probably spent at least an hour on your life today. What a great start – to have taken a good look at your life! Enjoy the insights that you found from the exercises. Blow your candle out when you are done for the day and come back tomorrow.

TIP: Remember your daily ritual as you enjoy your personal hour of power.

1. Light your candle.
2. Do your gratitude journaling of 12 things.
3. Assess the rating of your "inner fire" and take a small action to increase it.
4. Complete the next step of self-work outlined in the exercise that follows.
5. Blow out your candle when you're done.

DO YOU WANT TO SHARE?

How does it feel to look at your life this way? What have you learned about yourself from doing the cycle of life exercise? Please join the online community (the details are on page 22) and let me know.

STEP 2:
Dare to ask

"Feedback is the breakfast of champions."
Ken Blanchard

Today is all about going a layer deeper in your self-understanding and asking eight to 10 people who you know and, most importantly, whose opinions, values and attitude you deeply trust and respect, for their input. Choose wisely, even if it's a little scary to ask them.

These people may not necessarily be a family member or your partner if you feel that relationship isn't held sacred right now. You might not even choose the person

you consider to be your closest friend. You need people who value your place in the world and want to see you succeed. It could be anyone, such as:
- a family member
- friends
- a colleague, boss or mentor
- staff
- someone from your community or church
- a social club member
- a new friend

Choosing the right people for this feedback is key to your growth. You will have to trust your judgment on this one.

I suggest that you ask them the following questions using this kind of foreword:

Hi, I am currently doing some inner self-reflection work to transform my life and would value your constructive (i.e. honest yet kind) input into my life:

1. What do you consider my three top strengths in life?
2. What three things do you respect the most about me and how I show up in the world?
3. What do you consider my main weakness?
4. Do you ever see me falling into a pattern that I appear blind to? Which one of the following five might you intuit is the biggest default pattern that has tripped me up?
   - I give up too easily.
   - I push too hard for everything.
   - I lack self-worth.
   - I don't listen to my inner guidance and second guess myself.
   - I keep repeating the same mistakes and never integrate the lessons.
5. If you were able to give me two pieces of advice or insight on any topic in life, what would you most want me to know?
6. What book would you recommend I read and why?
7. What film would you recommend I watch and why?

I appreciate your honesty. Please can you get this back to me in two days.
Thank you.

Phew! How are you feeling just reading those questions?

Make a list right now of the eight to 10 people and, without even thinking about it, send those SMSs and e-mails or make the calls.

NOW!

How did it feel to ask for this feedback? Please tell me on the Facebook group. The details are on page 22.

Then you can blow your candle out.

STEP 3:
Find a different perspective

"A wise man never loses anything, if he has himself."
Michel de Montaigne

In the cycle of life exercise in Step 1, you wrote about your current life, looking for connections between the eight areas of your life. Today you are going to write some more about your life, but from a different perspective.

Every single one of us has a "wise self" – someone inside of us who is always there to guide us if we listen, who is all-knowing and will always help us make the right choices. It's an aspect of ourselves that is there, no matter what. We may not always listen to it or even acknowledge it, but it's there.

Do you believe in that higher, wise self, or is your life a bit of a mess that doesn't seem to have any wisdom lurking in it at all?

After your daily ritual, write the following in your journal:

> If I am deeply honest with myself and tap into my wiser self, which always has great insight into and understanding of me and my choices, what that wise aspect of me would want to share with the current me about my life is the following:

....

Then proceed to write about the eight areas of your life from that perspective.

It may help to have some delicious tea (or any drink of your choice) and calming music that uplifts your senses while writing.

It is normal to feel that this is weird. Just start writing and let it flow. You have nothing to lose, and you will be amazed at what comes out of your hand and into your journal. Let yourself write whatever comes to you about each of the eight areas, looking for patterns, insights, connections and answers for yourself.

Let this be easy!

Do you want to share what you have discovered? Please tell me on the Facebook group. The details are on page 22.

LIVE THE QUESTIONS NOW

*I would like to beg you, dear Sir, as well as I can,
to have patience with everything unresolved in your heart
and to try to love the questions themselves
as if they were locked rooms
or books written in a very foreign language.*

*Don't search for the answers, which could not be given to you now,
because you would not be able to live them.
And the point is to live everything.*

*Live the questions now.
Perhaps then, someday far in the future,
you will gradually,
without even noticing it,
live your way into the answer.*

Rainer Maria Rilke, *Letters to a Young Poet* (Vintage 1986), translation by Stephen Mitchell

STEP 4:
Get to grips with your glitch

Before we get stuck into this wonderful and exciting phase, in which you decide what shifts you want to make in your life and we unpack the five glitches, we need to check in with the people you asked for feedback.

If you haven't heard back from them yet, chase them up today so that you have those insights about yourself from your trusted sources. Call them up if need be.

CLIENT INSPIRATION
I am so blessed to have come into contact with Kate Emmerson when I was going through some huge changes, facing massive challenges and not knowing where to turn. As a mom of five children on the brink of adolescence, with a sick husband, and suffering immensely under the strain of life, I was desperate to find help and learn how to cope. I came across a small advert and contacted Kate.

From my first phone call with Kate, I knew I had found the right person to help me face these challenges. She changed my perspective on how I viewed life. I was so stuck in perfection, self-loathing, self-doubt and self-hate. My self-limiting beliefs were the hardest to get through. I felt trapped but Kate helped me understand how to change that.

Through a continual process of learning to love myself, taking stock of what is, facing fears and cutting through the layers I enrobed myself with, Kate made me aware of another way to deal with these stresses. It was the most liberating, powerful feeling.

I have since faced and dealt with one of my children going through three addiction rehabilitation centers. I have had the courage and strength of self-love to face my husband being diagnosed with a life-threatening brain tumor, him losing his ability to work and then the caring for him. I was responsible for managing and ultimately selling the business we had built up over three decades. I had tools to help me cope with selling properties, relocating to another province, and setting up a new home. I now know how to find my inner flame that allows me to ignite and reignite my life.

I am forever grateful to Kate for her positive, bubbly, passionate and infectious personal vibe that continues to inspire me.

Lyneth

DICTIONARY DEFINITION OF GLITCH

Before we can even contemplate ditching what it is that's holding us back, we have to have a better understanding of this term, and how it may present itself in our lives.

> GLITCH: A defect or malfunction in a machine or plan. A brief or sudden interruption or surge in voltage in an electrical circuit. *Computers:* any error, malfunction or problem.
>
> **Origin of word**
> 1962, American English, possibly from Yiddish *glitsh* "a slip", from *glitshn* "to slip", from German *glitschen*, and related *gleiten* "to glide". Perhaps directly from German; it began as technical jargon in the argot of electronic hardware engineers, popularized and given a broader meaning by the US space program.
> *From Dictionary.com*

For the purposes of this book, and more importantly your life, when I refer to the concept of "glitch", I am referring to anything that will stop your life from running smoothly – so in a sense a loose connection, a wonky wire, an energetic constriction. It could also be the way we hold our body to unconsciously protect ourselves, inadvertently constricting our breathing, or a pattern that we repeat habitually in our lives.

These glitches are the themes in our life that come out to "play" when we least want, need or expect them. Pesky things, these glitches are!

In fact, every time they rear their ugly heads, we seem to have forgotten that they were ever present before. (Remember my rabbits and how delusional I was about what was happening?) We often proclaim loudly, "I can't believe I'm in this same situation again." We wail, "Look what they have done to me!"

It can be around the topic of money, relationships, bosses, boundaries, doctors, lawyers, banks, health – you name it, we will claim to be the victim of it. In short, our glitches are our personal sabotaging mechanisms.

In NLP (Neurolinguistic Programming) training, there are a number of presuppositions, which are by definition statements that are taken for granted or assumed, that help us "frame" behavior and personal worth. One of them that is relevant here is: "All behavior has a positive intention".

Now when it comes to things like crime, murder, abuse, suicide and betrayal, you might resist that statement, but if you dig deeply, you will always find that someone is simply trying to make themselves feel better, needed and loved, and they may be behaving in a way that is not acceptable. I am saying that the intention underneath the behavior is always positive.

See how this client explains her own sabotaging behavior, which was tripping up her business.

CLIENT INSPIRATION
I was making great progress re-designing my business through coaching with Kate, letting go of aspects of it that were keeping me from moving forward. I was starting to make time for myself and take control of all eight aspects of my life again, but the one area I was continually struggling with was my cash flow. I just could not seem to get on top of the money. It was causing me major stress. I was buying stuff I didn't need, using vital cash flow inappropriately.

Kate suggested going deeper, using an NLP process, to see if there was an older memory that was holding this pattern hostage. Through a simple process led by Kate, I spontaneously found a memory from when I was a young teen. I was with my mom in a local supermarket and wanted a hairbrush that was pretty. My mom said that I didn't need it and that I had a brush at home. My parents were struggling financially at the time.

Gosh, what a memory! It was painful and made me so tearful, yet I was able to realize that I was still trying to keep the young girl in me happy. I was trying to make up for the disappointment and feelings of unworthiness by spending excessively and giving in to the young girl who had been so hurt by not having that brush.
TDP

WHAT'S YOUR INTENTION?

Can you see how obvious the link is? At the present-day adult level, TDP was overspending (the behavior), causing havoc in her life, all while trying to satisfy her younger self (positive intention).

It is useful in your own life to separate the intention from the behavior, so that we can add more appropriate behaviors to satisfy the same intention or underlying pattern. Too often we simply judge the behavior as wrong, inappropriate or damaging.

So this translates to the idea that no matter how crazy and destructive our own personal sabotage mechanism – our glitch – may be, at a deeper level, it is "acting out" to protect us and satisfy some yearning or need we have.

A client will come to me and say, "I don't want this life, addiction, lack of money, stress, bad health, shoddy relationship, people walking all over me, no motivation in life, busy-ness…" Yet they will keep repeating the same glitch pattern over and over again, all the while saying, "I don't want it".

So I will ask my client, "Well, how could this possibly be serving you? How could it be fulfilling something deeper?"

"No Kate, it's not, that's why I'm here talking to you and reading this book!"

We do not like to admit that something that appears negative is, in fact, working for us. It seems counterintuitive. Our job when working together and going through this book is to uncover how and why this particular glitch IS serving you.

Every time you say, "Well, it doesn't serve me", you are not serving yourself at the highest level. When we utter the words, "I don't know", we are yelling to the universe that we do not want to know, don't care to know or can't be bothered to know. It's often easier and more comfortable to sit in the trough of ignorance and denial.

Remember the four most dangerous words, "Oh, I know that!" They slam the door of possibility shut.

WAITING FOR THE ANSWERS

A well-developed emotional quotient (EQ) means you can go within and attempt to answer the questions, no matter how difficult or challenging they are.

The answers and insights will often come in the gaps between the words or questions. Your biggest growth can come while you are waiting for the answer.

Can you feel the difference between, "I don't know" and when you start to ask one of the following?

- How does this serve me?
- How could this possibly be serving me even though I don't like it?
- How is this supporting something else in my life?
- How is this reflecting something I'm terrified to admit?
- How is this linked to an old memory or pain?
- How is this giving me exactly what I need at some level right now?

Until you can begin to uncover the link, it will be pretty much impossible to release and heal. The glitch will win. We give our glitch total power and control, often subconsciously. What happens is that the glitch is simply responding to an inner impulse, and like a self-limiting belief, which we chat more about later in the book, the inner impulse will always win.

MAKING FRIENDS WITH YOUR GLITCH

What we do in our life, even when it is supposedly negative, somehow protects and supports us. Through our glitch, we play out deep-seated fears, longings, and mistakes, often in ways that are not healthy for our whole self.

We might say:
- I hate biting my nails.
- I don't like eating food so quickly.
- I don't like getting angry when my lover doesn't call at the right time.
- I don't like it – whatever it happens to be.
- I'm not motivated to go to gym but I know I should.
- I know I should have work-life balance.
- My life is a mess.
- My finances (or something else) are a total mess.
- My house is disorganized.
- My desk is in chaos.
- I'm always late.

We say that we don't like these things and want to change them, and we probably do, but what we don't recognize is the fact that not taking action to change these things is at some level working for us. So we need to befriend them before we can work through them. Fighting them won't change them.

I totally get that this can be a difficult concept to embrace. I fought like a wild cat when I first started taking responsibility, as I preferred playing in little girl mode. But then I got excited that I held the key to my own freedom. I could no longer be the victim and I had to choose to stand up and be counted.

When you do this, a total rebirth takes place. You get a fresh start, a new beginning. My wish for you is that you start taking full responsibility for everything in your life – and you'll learn how to do that through this book.

If you need to go and make a cup of coffee or tea and sit somewhere quietly to ponder this, off you go. Come back when you are ready.

THE UNIVERSAL GLITCHES

In my experience (which includes a BA degree in industrial psychology and human geography, working in the hospitality industry, and over 24 years of transformational work in the fields of aromatherapy, reflexology, meditation, stress management, energy healing, life coaching, NLP and EFT) I have realized that our glitches are universal and have five different kinds of underlying energy.

While it may seem a tad oversimplified, I do this on purpose. I know that making things complicated and intellectual can help to keep us stuck in our glitch – the antithesis of my aim. If we can keep something to a simple outline and a clear concept, it can be much easier to grasp, to relate to and thus to practically use to transform your life. Effective doesn't have to be complicated.

As you read about these glitches, you will recognize yourself in one, or perhaps a combination, of them. In fact, I will put money on the fact that you will have uncovered exactly what your glitch is through your own insights into the eight areas of your life in the very first exercise, along with the feedback from the people you respect, and expanded upon in the letter your wrote to yourself from your wise self.

Each glitch has a short overview, followed by six pointers on how it typically shows up in your world. Then I share nine common feelings you may experience and actual words you may utter if this is your particular glitch. Next, I offer up three ideas or concepts to consider embracing, and some practical ideas about physical exercise that will help you transform this glitch.

Glitch 1: Hopeless, helpless and hapless

> *"Most of the important things in the world have been accomplished by people who kept on trying when there seemed to be no hope at all."*
> Dale Carnegie

If this is your pet glitch, it typically rears its head when you lose hope and give up too easily. You tend to withdraw, burying your head in the sand and feeling desperately helpless and disempowered. You appear to lack tenacity and inner strength.

If you have learned to run when the going gets even slightly tough, you will have lost faith in your innate abilities, justifying why things won't work, no matter what you try. You lose the grit and determination required to push through just when you need it.

How does this show up in your world?
- Other people's opinions are way too important and have more weight than your own.
- You might be secretly jealous of what others have in life – be it their job, money, partner, cellphone, fabulous holiday – and you think they are lucky while you are not.
- You may be inclined to allow the past to dictate your future. Negative self-limiting beliefs chip away at you constantly and you draw on all the past experiences where you gave up.
- This glitch lacks hope and inspiration at every turn.
- You appear to be apathetic and resigned to life (often with sore hips and legs). "It will never change," you think, "there's no point. I'll never get anywhere."
- You regularly say you will do something and then renege on it, especially when it comes to your commitments to yourself.

Common words and feelings
- I can't.
- It will never work.
- I don't know how to.
- I'm too tired to think about it.
- It's too scary to think about.
- It will never change.
- What's the point?
- I don't really want it.
- What's on TV?

How can you show up courageously?
- Embrace your resilience and inner strength.
- Transform self-limiting beliefs.
- Don't allow your past to dictate your present and future.

Physical exercise
Choose exercises that will strengthen and connect you to your inner core, and also ones that will push your emotional boundaries and help you face stuff rather than running away.
- pilates
- biokinetics
- kettle bells
- yoga

- ballet
- weight training
- martial arts
- all adrenalin sports – paragliding, bungee jumping, rap jumping, high-speed boats, racing cars, water sports, shark diving. Anything that makes you face your fear.

CLIENT INSPIRATION
Recently on a retreat I chose a word from a series of random cards. The word was SHAME.

We were asked to intuitively decide where in our home this specific energy sat. At first I didn't understand – I hate the word and pretended to not get it. Kate pressed me to feel where the energy sat in my home, and I blurted out, "bed". It surprised me and I had to think about how and why this connection was there.

Where was the connection to my personal life regarding relationships, sex, family and the current events transpiring in my life?

I can now see that it is about wanting to block out stuff when it gets difficult. I take myself to bed.

The word "shame" is more about pity and feeling sorry for myself. "Shame, that's tough." It's about not dealing with what's going on. It allows me to switch off.
MB

Glitch 2: Pushy, pushier, pushiest

> *"How to succeed: Try hard enough. How to fail: Try too hard."*
> Malcolm S. Forbes

This glitch is for those who get stuff done, are five-million percent effective, always get their own way, and are so formidable that they usually walk over others to make things happen. They will fight with people and the universe about anything and everything.

Heaven forbid that you should ever take a breather and let your hair down – how imperfect of you!

How does this show up in your world?
- You typically force things to happen and control your and everyone else's actions.
- There is no room for the magic of possibility or for error.
- You always feel chased and are constantly being busy.
- You swim relentlessly upstream, making everything hard, rather than flowing effortlessly downstream.
- You can ruin relationships in your quest to perform and achieve.
- You might suffer from adrenal burnout, stress and immune disorders.

Common words and feelings
- I can do it better than anyone.
- I don't trust anyone.
- People always let me down.
- I do it faster and better, so why ask anyone?

- No one is ever there for me.
- I never have any time for myself.
- They are so lazy.
- I'll do it.
- There is never enough time in the day.

How can you show up authentically?
- Trust in the natural ebb and flow of life and the cycle you are in.
- Release the idea that busy is right.
- Allow yourself to increase true balance in your life.

Physical exercise
Typically you choose exercises that are very, very high energy and quite serious, so try activities that force you to chill out, slow down and have fun.
- walks on the beach
- gentle hikes
- yoga
- Tai Chi
- golf
- playing with kids on trampolines
- dancing
- fishing

Glitch 3: Worthless worth

"When you please others in hopes of being accepted, you lose your self-worth in the process."
Dave Pelzer

This is the über glitch, the one that underpins all the others. In my experience with clients and my own life, it is this one that will usually be rock bottom, and typically underpin one of the other four for a double whammy.

This draws on every time of your life when you somehow interpreted yourself to be "not good enough". It's your childhood, school, tertiary education, career, lovers, partnerships, decisions, ability to trust yourself, where you did or didn't grow up, what you learned about your value as a human being, what you believed about the feedback you got. It comes at you from all angles.

"Often those that criticize others reveal what he himself lacks."
Shannon L. Alder

How does this show up in your world?
- Every choice you make comes from a place of feeling deeply inferior.
- You play small. "Don't worry about little old me."

- You put others first in a way that is detrimental to yourself.
- You constantly accept second best and feel angry and resentful.
- Your boundaries are shoddy. You can't ask for what you really want or say no.
- You don't believe you deserve what you want and feel insignificant.

Common words and feelings
- I'm not good enough.
- They deserve it more than I do.
- It's selfish to ask for anything.
- Don't worry about me.
- It's okay; you go ahead and do "XYZ", I'll just stay at home.
- I don't deserve happiness or wealth.
- I can't go for that promotion.
- They would never be interested in me.
- I have nothing to say.

How can you claim your value and space in the world?
- Just being here makes me worthy, like everyone else.
- I am enough. I am no better or worse than anyone else. We are all as deserving as each other and I am included on that list.
- It is okay to put myself on my own priority list.

Physical exercise
Choosing any activity that you naturally enjoy or loved as a child is one of the fastest ways to build your self-worth and belief in yourself. It doesn't matter how off-the-wall or straight-laced it is. You could go from pole dancing to regular gym for this glitch. Our bodies are designed to move and you will release endorphins, dopamine and all the other good chemicals by getting off your butt. So just pick anything; enlist a friend or pay a personal trainer to keep you committed.

You will also benefit from having clearly defined goals, such as training for 30 days to walk 5 km. Achieving those will inch up your self-belief.

CLIENT INSPIRATION
Never feeling good enough deep down stems from being in an emotionally abusive relationship for way too long. I thought I should stay for the sake of the kids, when in fact the best thing I ever did for my kids was walk away and start again. When I allow others to degrade and disregard my worth, I give away a piece of my soul. We are all worthy of love, respect, happiness and the freedom to be who we are. We need to embrace and believe that and never let anyone devalue us.
Jen

My story
This was my biggest glitch too. Remember my story about my lack of self-worth showing up as bulimia? It has showed up in several ways throughout my life,

especially when I question my intrinsic value, no matter how small the "event". I recall my dad coming home from work one day with two copies of a book on how to make money, one for each of my brothers.

I felt so left out, so undermined, so unimportant that I wasn't given the same book. I felt hurt to my core. It might seem silly, but that was my response at the time. I was so wounded and pissed off that I went out and bought my own copy, but I carried those emotions around for a long time. The stuff we hold on to becomes real for us.

I was grappling with:
- I'm not good enough.
- I don't measure up to my brothers.
- I'm not important. I don't exist.
- I will never need to know how to make money.
- Women are different to men in our family.

And so it went on and on in my head. It was not a big event, yet it locked itself into my cells.

I could have turned around and thought, "Well, I know exactly what I'm doing with my money and have entrepreneurial ability, so Dad doesn't think I even need the book, just the boys do." That would be the thought of someone with stronger self-belief.

Glitch 4: Dreadful dismisser

> *"Your time is limited, so don't waste it living someone else's life. Don't be trapped by dogma – which is living with the results of other people's thinking. Don't let the noise of others' opinions drown out your own inner voice. And most important, have the courage to follow your heart and intuition."*
> Steve Jobs

This glitch shows up when you don't trust your deepest, innermost hunches, thoughts, ideas and feelings. You have had them bashed out of you, so you take someone else's opinion as more important than your own. Or you make logic and intellect rule over your heart and spirit. You constantly second guess your hunches and live with distrust of your own guidance.

How does this show up in your world?
- You ignore what you feel and don't understand the difference between excitement and fear.
- You hear the message, then find some way to override it, usually with logical thinking.
- You've been told not to trust what you feel.
- You think it can't be as easy as the messages you receive.
- You pooh-pooh the intuitive guidance you receive.
- You do everything to shut up the voice that lives inside you and quietly guides you, and go on at odds with your life.

Common words and feelings
- This can't be true, I'll check with someone else.
- I could never take action on that.
- I can't follow my dreams.
- I can't speak up – they won't believe me.
- They know better, so I'll keep quiet about what I'm sensing.
- If I do this, someone will get hurt.
- It's not the right time.
- I really shouldn't be doing this… but I will anyway.
- They know better than me.

How can you start listening to yourself?
- What I feel is valid and important.
- I can learn to trust my inner feelings, thoughts and desires and act on them.
- I am divinely guided in every moment.

Physical exercise
Choose activities in which you need to listen to and trust your body for balance and precision, or to just simply let you go wild.
- yoga (Bikram yoga requires internal concentration, and yin yoga strengthens intuition)
- boxing
- ice skating
- roller blading
- hiking in very hilly, tricky areas
- skiing
- biodanza
- NIA dancing
- free-form dancing where no one is watching (yes, you can go clubbing)

Or simply pick something that everyone has been telling you not to do, but that you know you want to.

Glitch 5: Bang bang

> *"The important thing is to learn a lesson every time you lose. Life is a learning process and you have to try to learn what's best for you. Let me tell you, life is not fun when you're banging your head against a brick wall all the time."*
> John McEnroe

If this is your baby, then you just bang, bang, bang your head against that same wall, time and time again. It's like you swallow "I-can't-remember pills" and you refuse to believe you have ever been in this situation before, so how can you possibly be going through this again?

You exasperate yourself and everyone around you. You do not join the dots between the same themes playing out in every area of life, and keep making the same poor choices over and over. This glitch is all about not integrating lessons learned.

CLIENT INSPIRATION
I sometimes repeat the same mistakes, which are mainly feeling guilty when I try to be more assertive or when I'm seeking out new dimensions. Luckily, I get a wake-up call from my inner voice and Kate and come back again.
Eleni

How does this show up in your world?
- You keep playing the same stuck record.
- You can't see your blind spots, as you don't know they are there.
- You blame others for everything in your life.
- The same theme keeps playing out in different areas of your life.
- You keep complaining and moaning rather than changing things.
- You ask people for advice but never take it.

Common words and feelings
- Oh my goodness, I'm here again. How did this happen?
- If I just try one more time…
- I can't let go just yet.
- I know things will be different this time.
- It will never happen again.
- I know better now.
- If only they didn't do the same thing.
- I'm sure this person will be different this time around.
- I can't help it, I just have to.

How can you apply wisdom?
- It's okay to let go of the old way of doing things.
- It's safe to learn new behaviors.
- I can get help and ask for support to find new ways of taking action.

Physical exercise
Choose activities that you have never tried before – that's it. Go mad and try out something exciting from your bucket list rather than doing the same old stuff.

I dare you to let go of any exercise you have been banging your head against and let yourself try something totally new. Just for three months. Why not?

If you have no idea what to do, make a list of things you have never tried and pick one.

TIME TO REFLECT

Now that you have identified your glitch (or glitches), we will be able to work with them and transform them step by step with this book.

Right now, take some quiet time to write down any of the statements, feelings or ideas that instantly resonated with you, so you have them on hand in your journal. You could also note any reactions you had to the above, in any way, and journal about how your particular glitch has played out in your life, using the above as guidelines.

You can share your new insights with the online community and be inspired by how other people are coming to terms with their glitches. The details are on page 22.

When you are done, blow out your candle, grab some water to rehydrate and enjoy the rest of your day.

Part two
Stepping up

Now that you have completed the first part, stepping in, we shift energetically to stepping up. You have the foundation of understanding where you are in life, so it's time to decide what's next for you.

This section is about expansion, being bolder, braver, bigger and more in all areas of life. Note this is not just about making more money or getting a better career: this involves your essence, spirit and self-development. For the purposes of working through the book and to get started, you will focus on stepping up in three areas of life, but there will be a knock-on effect in the rest of your life, as your awareness about everything will be heightened. It's time to ask for more and to believe you deserve more.

This section is packed with practical step-by-step tools and exercises to exponentially shift your life.

My story

After I had finished my coaching training in the UK and I was getting ready to come back to South Africa to start this grand business as a professional life coach, I started thinking about the image I wanted to portray. I had always worn loose, casual, flowing clothes, mostly because they hid my body and I had history of body stuff. My mum and I went to a fabulous department store that was having a sale, where I saw a beautiful, elegant, lilac silk and linen ladies' suit. It had lined trousers and a beautifully cut jacket. When I tried it on I felt like a business goddess. Funny how clothes can do that, hey?

I realized the value of having something special in one's wardrobe. Until that moment I hadn't really thought about brand and image and how people would take me seriously in my business. It was an hour in my life when I stepped up to something bigger than I was used to, something bolder. My mum bought the suit for me as a Christmas gift. Things that can be so ordinary for you can be profound for someone else.

About three months later, when I was back in Johannesburg, my mum came out to visit and I was waiting for her at the airport. I saw a woman who was also waiting, and I could not take my eyes off her. She was just glowing. I'm not talking about her looks or her clothes. Everything about her oozed serenity, power, ease and grace. I was mesmerized by her "energy". I have always trusted myself to act on things I feel, so I walked up to her and told her she looked truly beautiful. She turned to me with tears in her eyes and said she was in the midst of a divorce and that my comment was just what she needed to hear.

She told me she worked part-time at a well-known business magazine in Johannesburg, and that she was going to get me an interview to help me get known. True to her word, a few weeks later I was being interviewed and photographed. I wore those beautiful lined lilac trousers with an elegant blouse (it was too hot for the jacket) and felt like a million bucks!

I had stepped up and things shifted.

STEP 5:
Envision your future

"Your vision will become clear only when you can look into your own heart. Who looks outside, dreams; who looks inside, awakes."
Carl Jung

You deserve a treat – something fun and playful yet utterly profound. You have spent heaps of time and energy delving into yourself.

When you were a child, did you ever play with huge pieces of cardboard, piles of magazines, sticky gummy glue, glitter, crayons and kokis, simply dreaming and envisioning your inner world, or stuff you fantasized about? You would cut out pictures and paste them however you felt inspired to and you knew exactly that you were manifesting your dreams in visual form. What bliss! What fun! What power!

As adults we tend to forget the power we held as children. We have learned to become more serious, perhaps more dull, reducing the amount of time we allow ourselves to play, to be free, to dream. We have responsibilities, demands, work, and commitments, dammit.

We need to shed the idea of, "I'm too old for this. What a load of rubbish, Kate!" If you have never created a vision board, you may be tempted to skip this step. Stop and let me explain why you should do it.

Go back to your commitment form and remember that you agreed to attempt everything that I send your way in this book. Perhaps this is one exercise that you are questioning the validity of right now. It will take you a couple of hours of your life and if you have a partner, relatives or kids living with you, why not get everyone involved in this fun, engaging and enlightening process?

I have a client, Adré in Somerset West, who was so delighted by vision boards that she decided to give this wonderful process, facilitated by me in her home, to her closest family and friends as their birthday present for the year, no matter when their birthday was. They are now committed to helping each other make their vision boards come to life and they meet to connect about what action they have taken in life towards their dreams. That is powerful!

SPEAK TO YOUR HEART

Your vision board is all about intention. When people ask me if I can give them one piece of advice about how to make shifts in life, I tell them it all starts with your real, conscious intention. It can override everything, overcome obstacles and keep every single thing that you think, do, feel and experience aligned on one target.

Your vision board helps you to envision your future. You can create a board for your entire life, or it can be for one specific area that is your main focus. I recommend making a vision board every year. At first I created them irregularly, but now I have been doing them for the last three years, and my life has shifted exponentially since then.

In the toolkit section (see page 23), I gave a list of everything that you need to create your vision board. If you haven't managed to do that yet, perhaps you should go on a shopping spree today or raid your kids' rooms. This is what you are looking for:

- Cardboard: I usually like A1 size, but have done them on A2 as well. Some clients have even made bigger ones. You could even do it in your journal, giving a page to each area of your life. If you want something sturdier, use triplex board. Make it your own.
- Glue.
- Scissor.
- Glitter.
- Crayons or kokis.
- Stickers – I love stars and hearts.
- Wide selection of magazines: Do you know the saying "a picture is worth a thousand words"? Well, this is what you are doing – speaking to your heart and soul in a visual format. Think back to the eight areas of life and make sure you can cover all those aspects by choosing different types of magazines, such as finances, lifestyle, travel (pop into a travel agent to get brochures), career, spirituality, health, psychology, glitz and glam, techie stuff, cars and anything else that tickles your fancy. If you are doing this wonderful process with others, I recommend that you each bring about eight to 10 magazines and then share them around.

"Vision without action is a dream. Action without vision is simply passing the time. Action with vision is making a positive difference."
Joel Barker

My story

I will never forget my second vision board 10 years ago. To be different, I did it on black cardboard (the previous year's had been on white). It was the year I decided I wanted to move from Johannesburg to Cape Town. I found an incredible picture that included blue sky, Table Mountain, the 12 Apostles Hotel (one of my favorite spots), some boulders and the gorgeous sea.

I had no idea how I was going to do the move. I met a love interest that January, told her I was planning to move to Cape Town, and just eight months later we relocated together, with four animals in tow.

My vision board, being precious and big, was the last item to go in the boot of the car, carefully rolled up, on top of luggage, blankets and pillows. Sixteen hours later, after the mammoth cross-country trek, we opened the boot and pulled the vision board out first. I kid you not, when I got inside and unrolled it, that very picture of the mountain and sea had fallen off it. Goosebumps! It was done. I will never forget that moment.

2014 was another very powerful year for me. I had chosen some very big things to manifest in my year ahead, and went bold on my board. The main theme was "global nomad" and "a decadent odyssey". I love to travel for work and play. I had no trips overseas booked yet, but by the close of 2014 I had traveled six times for international speaking engagements, and once to take my mum to Mauritius. It was insanely delightful.

I had also put a picture of four currencies on my board: pounds, dollars, yen and euros. I had earned money in pounds before, but never those other currencies.

My first trip, to Warsaw, was in March, and I was told, "Katey, our head office is in the USA. Can we pay you in dollars?" Yes, please!

A while later I was invited first to Cyprus and then a couple of months later to Saudi Arabia by the same group that took me to Warsaw. "Kate, we need to pay you in euros, is that okay?" Yes, thank you!

I also work regularly with a London-based client, which meant my pound pot was being filled.

Still no yen, but I'm not complaining. The saying "shoot for the moon and you'll land among the stars" holds very, very true.

One more personal story, as it's just so profound for me. My favorite online course I have put together is called "Shift Your Property" and it helps clients to let go of their emotional attachment to a home before selling it, as well as decluttering to make the packing and move easier. I do loads of this practical work all the time with face-to-face clients and got great reviews from people testing the course, but I had not sold one single copy of the course. I decided to put the cover of the course on my board. Within five and a half weeks, a local company had bought 100 copies of that course!

WHY IT WORKS

Making a vision board requires only a few hours of your life, it's fun, and it holds the possibility of ditching your glitch, igniting your fire and living your dream. What have you got to lose? But if you still need more convincing, this is why they work.

The law of attraction

You are giving time and energy to that which you want to manifest, which keeps your desires uppermost in your mind. If you look at your vision board daily for inspiration, your attention will be focused on positive goals. Seeing your desires motivates you to achieve them. If you need an extra push, share your vision board with those who are close to you.

Your emotional body, which is behind the law of attraction, will respond to the images you see, and bring them to fruition. Jack Nicklaus, a world champion golfer, said, "I never hit a shot, not even in practice, without having a very sharp in-focus picture of it in my head."

Biological reasons

I love this explanation of the reticular activating system (RAS), which is part of your brain, by Stuart Warner of www.make-your-goals-happen.com.

He suggests that you imagine you're in an airport. It's full of people, noise, music and announcements. But you hear all that sound in the background and don't pay attention to most of it, especially not as individual sounds.

But if there's an announcement saying your name or flight number, your attention tunes in to it. This is your RAS kicking in. It's "like a filter between your conscious mind and your subconscious mind," Stuart writes. "It takes instructions from your conscious mind and passes them on to your subconscious. For example, the instruction might be, 'Listen out for anyone saying my name'."

When you create a vision board, you are telling your RAS to pay attention to your desires. And when you pay attention to them, you notice opportunities you can take to make them happen. It switches on your radar.

HOW TO CREATE YOUR VISIONARY VISION BOARD

The first thing is to put on some awesome music and get comfortable. Start by paging through magazines and cutting out any images, words, letters or ideas that jump out at you and inspire you. You can also use photographs, cards and gift tags. I had actual foreign currency stuck to my board. Anything goes!

You can cut out single letters to make up words, or include your favorite quote, inspirational messages and passages from books.

I like to make each year center on a theme. As I said, 2014 was "global nomad"; 2015 is "exponential leverage". You can borrow those if you want or come up with your own.

Be bold, big and daring. There's no playing small with your board. You can include things that represent the feelings, thoughts, words, possessions and experiences you wish to bring into your life. If you want a car, find the exact car you want. A healthy body? Put your head on top of a picture that inspires you. If you want an award of excellence, create a picture of you holding the award. Make it specific.

If you prefer to make your vision board digitally, there are apps that you can download. I have done that before, but personally I prefer the tangibility of making it with my hands and then converting it digitally. You have to try it out and see what resonates best for you.

PUT IT UP

Seeing your board often is essential, so it's best to put it up. If you live with a partner, try the inside of your clothes cupboard, or your own space in the house, like your craft room or study. Your office at work can be good, especially if it is a career or money board.

Look at your vision for life first thing in the morning and last thing at night. My physical board is up on a window so I can see it from my bed.

Take it a step further and make it your screen saver on your computer, phone or tablet – it is estimated that we unlock our phones on average 116 times per day. Last year was the first time I put mine on my phone, and it was the most inspirational year of my life. Is it my screen saver again? Hell, yeah!

Where have you put your vision board? Tell me online. The details for joining the community are on page 22.

CLIENT INSPIRATION

I joined one of Kate's vision board sessions in a very dark period in my life. I was coming out of an emotionally unstable marriage where I had lost all sense of self-worth and my zest for life.

I spent years sacrificing my dreams and happiness in an effort to please my partner, yet nothing was good enough for him. I allowed myself to be broken down so much that I even started believing the degrading labels and insults he constantly hurled at me. I fell into a cycle of self-pity and depression, neglected my business, withdrew from my friends, and pretty much gave up on life. But being a single mom of two beautiful children, I knew something needed to shift in my life.

I found a really cool focal statement for my vision board: "Jen's in charge!" I added: "Life isn't about finding yourself, it's about creating yourself." Then I included really meaty stuff to push myself, like "out of my comfort zone" and "she's a woman with a plan, she makes things happen". A big part of my vision board focused on healing myself with massages, solitude and meditation.

There were also the things I love to do, like travel, and the things I hoped to do with the words "my pen, my inspiration, my life – be creative". I was even bold enough to add "the legend lives on" and "I am eternal".

The vision board itself was almost overwhelming as for so long I hadn't been in charge of my own life, I had lost myself, and I had almost forgotten how to make things happen. I felt too guilty to spend time or money on myself.

I covered every inch of my board with stuff to push me forward, and I stuck it up in my bedroom so it was the first thing I saw every morning when I opened my eyes. I had pretty big things to live up to. A legend cannot exactly mope about feeling sorry for herself and the raw deal she has been dealt in life.

How has my vision board manifested in my life? Well, I am currently writing my book, which has been sitting in the back of my mind for the past eight years. I finally broke away from my toxic marriage, reclaiming my freedom and self-respect. I am also really focused on building my travel business and having the flexibility to work from home so that I can be more available to my beautiful children. And most importantly, I am loving and being good to me, and not feeling bad about that at all.

Having visuals and courageous statements really shifted things for me. When life bites at me, I simply ask, "How would a legend handle this?" and then I take charge in a way that serves both me and those involved in a positive manner."

Jen

STEP 6:
Ignite your cycle of life

"If you have built castles in the air, your work need not be lost; that is where they should be. Now put the foundations under them."
Henry David Thoreau, *Walden*

Before we go further, I want to check that every day you are still committing to your ritual of lighting your candle, gratitude journaling and the fire rating.

The next exercise is about choosing the three areas of your life you wish to activate and shift in the coming weeks.

I know that by answering all the questions in the cycle of life exercises you have really been giving all eight areas of life some applied thought. Isn't it amazing how just taking an honest look at everything can already start shifting things?

Rather than letting your fire die and allowing your glitch to win, you can use self-awareness and honesty to clear away the old ashes in preparation for a new fire. Your fire probably didn't go out overnight, so I applaud you for your courage and willingness to address this now, as it is going to be a process.

COMMIT TO THREE

Grab your journal or go back in the book to look at your diagram, re-read your answers to the cycle of life, and start making some decisions. You now have to pick three areas in your life to constructively work on by creating specific goals for them.

It is important to pick the three that really matter. Perhaps they are the ones where your glitch is currently tripping you up the most, wreaking havoc with other areas of life, or dampening your inner flame. It will be the areas causing you the most physical, emotional or mental distress.

Perhaps they are the three areas you worry about the most or the ones that dampen your flame endlessly. Maybe they are the ones you feel the most guilty about, as they will release so much fire energy when you regain control of them. Or perhaps these are the three areas that you always ignore in favor of other things, yet they are the ones that will truly make the biggest impact on your fire energy.

Trust your intuition when deciding which areas to commit to, no matter how scary it may seem.

SET A TIME FRAME

Decide when you wish to achieve some goals by. I suggest five weeks from now but you can choose any time frame. If there is a special date coming up, like your birthday, spring day or year end, choose one that feels right for you, as long as it is less than six weeks away, otherwise you are giving yourself too long, and you might lose heart. When clients do this as an online course, I make them commit to a specific date, five weeks from now.

Take a different colored pen to the one you used in the cycle of life exercise, and fill in a new outer boundary to represent the new percentage that you want to achieve in five weeks. Only do this for the three areas you have chosen.

See diagram 4 on page 149

You will have a visual of the gap between where you are right now and where you want to be by the end of this course. See if you can be bold enough to push the current percentage in your three chosen areas and double them. So if you've chosen fun and it's at 30% now, is it possible to commit to getting this slice up to 60% in the next few weeks? If home and family is an area you want to work on, and let's say it is now on 35%, could you commit to doubling it to 70%?

The only exception is that if an area you've chosen is currently sitting at 10% or lower, it's a cold dead spot in your fire, so I am going to challenge you to get this up to at least 30% within five weeks. It will have a huge positive impact in your life.

IT'S TOO MUCH!

If you feel that working towards goals in three areas of life is a bit over the top for you, you may choose to work on two areas. I would rather you work on two goals and achieve them than attempt three and fail them all.

This requires self-honesty. If you always let yourself off the hook and give up, I would suggest that you go for all three and push yourself to achieve them. You'll create real shifts and regain control over your life. If, however, you are generally pretty good at doing things that you say you will, yet at this time your life is extremely busy, perhaps two will be a great shift for now.

A warning: if you feel you are honestly playing small and letting yourself off the hook by opting for only two areas, you are letting your glitch win yet again. That's not a good enough reason. You need to go for three areas.

BRING IT TO LIFE

Now that you have chosen your three areas to ignite and re-drawn your cycle of life with the percentages you are committing to, we have to make your new percentages specific, clear and tangible, and word them as constructive goals.

Before we do this, please write a little in your journal about each of the three areas, and what you want to have accomplished in them within the five weeks.

Think from the end point, as if you are already five weeks down the line, and what you will have accomplished. How will your personal fire be burning when your new percentages are achieved? What will this area of life be like at this new percentage for you?

Using the previous example, for your fun to be at the new level of 60%, what is the end result or outcome that you would need to have? What goal will you have achieved so that you will know without a shadow of a doubt that you are sitting on 60%?

Be self-challenging. Playing small does not serve you, even though we are taking small, constructive steps to ignite our fires. So judge for yourself. In other words, to begin to make extraordinary steps towards a roaring, passionate fire, what do you know that you will have accomplished in five weeks? Your goal needs to be very clear, and needs to be the focus point you are working towards, like a GPS co-ordinate.

You might say, "Oh, I just want to be really happy." Well as vital as happiness is, it is very difficult to calculate and "tick off". It may be more useful to ask yourself what kind of things will make you happier and less stressed. Maybe you will have done a beginner's course in French or marketing; joined a salsa class; signed up with a personal trainer and lost two kilos; gone on a romantic weekend away with your partner…

Can you see how you need to think of something that is tangible that you can work towards that will change that area of life?

SET AWESOME GOALS

A goal is the outcome you wish to achieve in an area of life. Goals make a difference to you and give you something to strive towards IF they are meaningful. Achieving a goal is really the result of many, many tasks. When you are creating your goal, you are quite simply setting your destination. It is the same as when you go on a road trip – well, most of them anyway – you have a destination in mind.

Are you leaving Johannesburg and traveling to Durban or Cape Town? Or leaving London to go to San Francisco? You can't tell yourself, "I don't want to be in London". It will not get you anywhere. When setting goals, think of the destination of your journey; the target. The goal is not the journey itself – that is the part you still have to walk, the fun part too.

You may write your goal as "I will exercise three times a week". Well, as noble and challenging as that is, that is really a recurring action that you will have to do. Why are you exercising and what do you want to achieve by doing it?

The goal is the higher reward at the end of all your effort, such as lowering your body fat percentage and reaching your ideal weight, running a 10 km race or fitting into your favorite jeans again.

Read this again, as it is important.

You have to know what the end picture is. Why are you doing all this work and what is motivating you? If you wake up in the morning and don't feel like exercising because you are tired, it is easy to go back to sleep. However, if you have the goal of weighing 70 kilograms by your birthday party, the incentive is that much greater to get up and do what you need to.

> GOAL: "I weigh an energetic 70 kilos and am wearing my favorite jeans."
> ACTION: Exercise three times a week plus whatever else required.

Most of us make goals in the latter way, making long lists of actions and then wondering why we don't achieve them.

Now we take action

Action steps get you to your destination. On the road trip you have to travel mile after mile, fill up with petrol, oil and water, and re-fuel yourself with food and beverages. So if you do something on a regular basis, it is an action and not a goal. Ensure you know where the action will lead you so you can focus on the outcome or goal as an incentive.

Can you see the difference between a goal and action steps?

Often people think they have set goals and they have really just given themselves lists of to-do items. It's demotivating and exhausting as there's no end in sight.

Action steps are the little things that will take you step by step towards the goals. Every goal is made up of hundreds of actions, which lead to mini goals, which lead to bigger goals.

Action steps are:
- Determined by your goal.

- Usually repetitive.
- A combination of different actions that will get you to the final goal.
- The habits we create that help us towards the goal.

For example, action steps in line with the health goal above would be:
- Go to gym to strength train three times a week.
- Weigh myself weekly.
- Cut off the visible fat on food.
- Replace butter with olive oil.
- Drink three pints of water daily.
- Record everything I eat to observe my patterns and habits.
- Enjoy one meal a week with no restrictions.
- Restrict alcohol to the weekend.
- Re-program my thoughts by meditating every night.

SOME EXAMPLES

So, to get back to your practical exercise, think about the three areas and the goal or outcome that you are going to achieve.

Have a look at these good intentions versus well-formed goals:

"I hope to have dropped some weight this month…"
"Yeah, right", is what I reply because it just will not happen. You have to word it with the sense of power, knowing and achievement that it has already happened. Use the present tense (rather than future possibility) to elicit energy and motivation. When you state it as having already happened, your subconscious and conscious minds realize that you mean business.

Be concise and clear. Imagine that each word is worth a million bucks to you, so if the word is included it has to be super powerful. Add an emotion about how it will feel to have achieved the goal.

Have a goal date (this can be implied by the five-week time frame you have set, so you don't always have to state it).

See how much more effective this one is:

"I am so proud to weigh an energetic 70 kilos and to be wearing my favorite jeans at my book launch."

Don't you think that this wording will be much more effective and give you a higher chance of actually doing it? It's because you know exactly where you are headed and why.

"I want to be tidier."
Well it won't happen if you word it like that! Try this instead: "I love knowing where everything is in my home. I have decluttered my cupboard and my desk is organized."

"I want to look better."
Yes and? You have no way of knowing what you need to do to achieve this.
"I get complimented on my whole new look and hairstyle, and love my new glasses."

"I would like to be more productive and have more business."
Well, that's a great intention, and a very important one, but this statement will not help you. How will you know that you have been more productive and allocated your time and energy better?
"My business has grown an extra 10% with five new clients that have each spent R5 000."

Can you see that the way in which you word your goals creates a huge difference? A great goal automatically creates pictures in your mind of what it will look like when you achieve it. It is specific and you can tick it off as either accomplished or not. It has energy and motivation built into it and entices you to achieve it.

In practice, this can be quite challenging to do on your own, especially the first time. Can I support you? This is a great time to join the community if you haven't already. Mail shift@kate-emmerson.com to be invited to join.

"People say what we are all seeking is the meaning of life... I think what we're really seeking is the experience of being alive."
Rudyard Kipling

STEP 7:
Remind yourself

"Reality is a projection of your thoughts or the things you habitually think about."
Stephen Richards

Take your positive, powerful goals and write all three down anywhere and everywhere that you will see them.

Get some nice cards, cut cardboard to the right size or use Post-its, and put them on your desk, in your wallet, on your fridge, as a screen saver, by your bed, on your mirror, cupboard... Put them up wherever you will see them.

Think about where you spend a lot of time. If you are on the road, put them up in your car and in your purse. If you stay at home, use your fridge and mirrors. If you are stuck to your desk, then use your computer. Always keep them on you in some way, in your pockets and handbag. You need to read them over and over again.

Please also share them with our Facebook group. The details are on page 22.

TIP: Save them in your phone and set an alarm three times a day to remind yourself.

You need to re-energize and motivate yourself as much as possible by reading your goals. Ideally, seeing them should make you feel lighter and excited about the fact that you are working towards them, perhaps even a little scared and challenged too. If they don't lift your spirits and make you want to take positive action, go back to the previous step and think about re-stating them in a better way.

Now blow out your candle. You have done so well today!

STEP 8:
Get jiggy with your goals

> *"As I grow older I pay less attention to what men say. I just watch what they do."*
> Andrew Carnegie

I love this step, as now you will use your hour today to really unpack your three goals and make them more concrete, tangible and workable.

Grab something delicious to drink – I suggest water jazzed up with lemon, ginger, basil or orange slices – and complete all the following questions for your goals, one at a time.

WHY DO I REALLY WANT TO DO THIS?
If you are doing this goal for anyone else, may I politely suggest that you go back to the beginning and re-think it? This has to be something that you are in control of and you want to do for yourself, not because someone else wants you to. The latter will not give you an ounce of energy or motivation.

WHAT ARE THE POSITIVE BENEFITS OF ACHIEVING THIS GOAL?
Think about the significant impact it will have on you and those around you.

WHAT ARE THE NEGATIVE CONSEQUENCES OF NOT ACHIEVING THIS GOAL?
Be realistic and think about how you will feel if you come up short in five weeks.

WHAT RESOURCES DO I ALREADY HAVE TO HELP ME ACHIEVE THIS GOAL?
Resources are people, money, time, equipment, networks, skills, education, books, etc. Dig deep, as often things seem insurmountable yet we have so much at our disposal we take for granted. List them all.

WHAT RESOURCES DO I STILL NEED TO ASSIST ME TO ACHIEVE MY GOAL?
Think about the resources listed above. What are you missing?

WHAT ARE THE POTENTIAL OBSTACLES ALONG THE WAY?
Make a list of things you might fall prey to, like boredom, de-motivation, lack of time, work commitments, money, fear. These will be linked to your glitch.

WHAT'S A POTENTIAL SOLUTION FOR EACH OBSTACLE?
If I want this goal so badly, what will I have to do to make sure I am on top of these obstacles and not use them as an excuse at the end of the day?

Typically, finding solutions is hard. If you have a fitness goal, your potential obstacle might be that you won't get to gym. So we say that to overcome it, we'll go to gym. That is really an action, not a solution. Perhaps you should hire a personal trainer so you will not renege, join a club, or partner up with a friend for exercise. You have to be very specific to find a solution to an obstacle.

WHAT ARE MY THREE KEY STRENGTHS AND HOW CAN THEY ASSIST ME WITH THIS GOAL?
If you need some inspiration, take a look at the feedback you got from your trusted sources.

WHAT ARE THE MAIN ASPECTS OF THIS GOAL?
If it is a health goal it may encompass eating, drinking, exercise, medical check-ups, supplements, mind set and affirmations, handling eating out in restaurants, family support, etc.

WHO CAN I BE ACCOUNTABLE TO?
Am I willing to share this with someone to get their support, and when will I speak to them? Remember that the online community is a perfect place to share your goals and to be held accountable. The details are on page 22.

NOW FOR THE OTHER TWO
If you have the time and energy, repeat this exercise for goals two and three. Or you can do that in your hour tomorrow. I dare you to have fun with this!

STEP 9:
Make an action plan

"Do it, and then you will feel motivated to do it."
Zig Ziglar

How are you feeling now you have gotten jiggy with all three of you goals? If you still need to complete that, please do it before you start today's section.

You have found your three top goals to achieve over the next five weeks, and answered all those questions, so today you will create your action plan on paper. You may have done so during the process yesterday, but I am talking about having your actions on a sheet of paper, in your journal or on your calendar, so that they are easy to refer to.

This will back up your goals and make them 100% more achievable. I asked you to write out your original three goals and place them everywhere you can see them, and you also need to commit to your action steps visibly, so that each week will take you towards your bigger goals.

Goals without action will leave you disappointed, frustrated and without an ounce of fire in sight. We are here to ignite your flame, so keep your eye on the bonfire and take baby action steps to stoke it every single day.

Look at all your answers and insights from yesterday, and start making notes about how you are going to practically achieve what you need to each week. What phone calls, appointments, help and actions do you need to schedule so that you are on track?

Will Rogers said it best: "Even if you're on the right track, you'll get run over if you just sit there."

MONITOR YOURSELF

See action plan 1 on page 150

This action sheet offers a simple way for you to monitor your weekly action plan and have it in one place. You can use this in conjunction with your regular diary if you choose, if that works better for you, but often trying a new way can have a greater effect in helping you get things done. Do what works for you.

Fill in each goal you have created for this five-week period, then complete all the actions that will fall under each goal for this week only. Keep it visible: on the fridge, your desk or wherever you will see it often.

Complete your action plans today for the full week ahead, then complete another one for the following week and so on. There is a great rule for personal effectiveness called the 10/90 Rule (taken from Brian Tracy's book *Eat That Frog!*) that states: "The first 10% of time that you spend planning and organizing your work, before you begin, will save you as much as 90% of the time in getting the job done once you have started."

You can find more time in each day by simply planning. So get your plan completed so that you can get cracking with your action steps.

Notice that each goal also has a reward column at the end of it. It doesn't matter what day of the week your plan starts on, just let it run for seven days. Decide at the beginning of your week how you will reward yourself for each goal and all the corresponding actions you will have accomplished.

You could even set up a combined system for all three goals if you prefer, and for every single action that you can tick off for the week, you get a "point" or a "star". Every 10 points or stars equals your wonderful reward. Every 20 points equals a bigger reward.

Rewards are so important to create enthusiasm and to recognize all your determination and dedication. Make the rewards really exciting so that you want to enjoy them every week, eg. a massage, movie-dinner date, new book, visit gallery, etc.

My story

As I sit at my desk right now working on this book, I am under a lot of other deadlines and pressure, with several projects happening at once: I am crowd-funding to raise money to go to the USA (the day after I submit this book) to appear in a self-development movie, I am negotiating my own TV show based on *Clear Your Clutter* with the Home Channel, as well as running a Complete Your Book mastermind group for 11 writers.

Yikes! I admit it is a tad overwhelming at times. So planning, staying focused and looking after my energy levels have been my priorities. So too is making sure I totally switch off. My personal reward is dancing. (I took up salsa dancing after putting it on my vision board in 2014). So, meeting deadlines for all my projects means I can attend classes or dance the night away at a social. I also know that dancing totally frees up my brain and melts away stress as all I can focus on is the person I'm dancing with and my feet – and doing my darnedest to look sassy at the same time. I come back to my goals, actions and deadlines with renewed energy, even if my feet are sore.

IF YOU FAIL TO PLAN, THEN YOU PLAN TO FAIL

It is important to write things down so that you cannot con yourself into thinking you are making progress when, in fact, you aren't. We get good at that, don't we? When we start to let things slip, the danger is that we'll let everything slide past. That's why we record everything as we ditch our glitches.

Just like you have to vigilantly watch a fire so that it does not peter out, you also have to keep an eye on the changes you wish to make. It is so rewarding to notice everything you are doing. It spurs you on. On days where you might slack off, this plan will be your visual stimulus to get back on track the next day. It doesn't matter if you slip up, it matters that you keep at it, day after day, as best as you can.

TIP: Spend five minutes every morning looking at your vision board and your action plan to see what needs to be completed for the day. Come back to it again during the day and at night. Tick each item off daily to keep track.

So, now you have your plan mapped out, we can take the next little step to get even more control over your life.

What's your action plan? I'd love to know, so please share it with me on our Facebook group. The details are on page 22.

STEP 10:
Find your self-limiting beliefs

"Reality continues to ruin my life."
Bill Watterson, *The Complete Calvin and Hobbes*

Today I want to chat to you about your self-limiting beliefs. This is our glitch in action. The name says it all: we limit ourselves and we create this reality that can ruin our lives.

Those little self-doubting, self-berating, judgmental things we see, think, feel and believe about ourselves are our worst enemies when it comes to growth, change and moving out of our comfort zones. Self-limiting beliefs come in all sorts of disguises, and for the most part they are only true because we deem them to be.

Read that again.

A BUCKET OF ICE-COLD WATER

When we have adopted a belief (from our parents, teachers, ministers, siblings, authority figures, or simply made our own assumptions in response to the world around us) then it becomes an irrefutable fact for us. We don't question it and half the time we aren't even conscious that we hold that belief in the first place. But boy oh boy, do they wreak havoc! The beliefs are usually our glitches in action.

That voice pounds inside your head telling you that you're not good enough to get that job, will never find the right boyfriend or get fit, can't stand up and talk to a crowd, will never make a million rand, that you're too old… All the voice is doing is limiting your view of yourself and your world around you. If your belief was actually true, it would be true for everyone, and you know that is not the case.

So our beliefs are merely perceptions that become so deeply ingrained that they start running and ruining our lives. They're the biggest bucket of ice-cold water that we douse our fire with. When we take on a belief as our own, it is instantly fixed and immutable. They become the lens through which we view the world, the rules by which we live. They are very powerful – until you do an exercise like this and face them head on.

The beliefs that you hold will either work for or against you. The positive ones you hold are great; there is nothing we need to do with them. But the self-limiting beliefs are the "nurglies" that need weeding out.

For example, if you believe that you are not good enough, then it will cause you to re-create the same experiences over and over again. Just taking different actions in your life will not be enough to shift your life permanently. You have to change the underlying patterns too. It is the same as trying to treat acne from the outside only, when in actual fact it is the blood stream, immune system, skin layers, kidneys, stress and other things that are creating it. It's best to approach any problem from all sides. If you just treat the external, the gunk inside keeps showing up. Beliefs govern you from the inside out, so being able to make long-lasting changes requires a multi-pronged approach.

AN ENDLESS SPIRAL

Jack Canfield has a wonderful explanation of self-limiting beliefs in his book *The Success Principles* (HarperCollins Publishers, 2005). Here is an excerpt:

> *We get stuck in endless loops of re-enforcing behavior, which just keep us stuck in our downward spiral. The limiting thoughts/beliefs we have will create images in our minds, and these images govern our behavior, which in turn re-enforce the limiting thought. For example imagine thinking you are going to forget your lines for your next work presentation. That stimulates a thought of you forgetting a particular key point. This creates an experience of fear. This clouds your thinking and then true as anything it makes you forget one of your key points. This immediately re-enforces your self-talk that "I can't speak in front of groups. You see, I knew I would forget what I was meant to say." And then the limiting belief is just made deeper. Unless you find a way to start breaking that limiting belief, this will be your experience every single time, because of this loop that happens.*

This example illustrates that your belief then becomes your truth that you are a lousy speaker, and there is no way forward from that, you just believe it, and keep away from making a fool of yourself again.

While this is totally understandable and normal, is there a negative cost to this? You may now be resisting things out of fear of potential negative consequences. Remember that your glitch is simply trying to protect you in some way; in this case from being a fool and getting laughed off the stage. But what if you could actively change that? What if your talent lies in being able to get up and speak to an audience, and a couple of bad experiences have simply made you doubt yourself and your ability? That would be such a waste. A waste of your potential!

I guarantee that in your own life there will be limiting beliefs that you hold which are actively blocking your progress to a more successful and happy life.

GO DEEPER WITHIN

To make any headway towards your exciting new goals, you have got to start thinking, feeling and believing in line with what you want. This sounds quite hard but this process makes it easy.

The following are the three most important ways to create new outcomes, ignite your fire and achieve your goals in life.
- We can create new circumstances in life with powerful "imagining", using visualization and having visual images to gaze at and step into – this is your vision board.
- We can change our behavior to create new habits. This refers to your goals and the action steps you are taking towards them.

- This is the big one: we can go deeper within and address the underlying limiting beliefs that may have created our current circumstances and underpin all our actions. We must replace them with positive, powerful self-affirmations and self-talk. We are doing that today.

FINDING YOUR LIMITS

Go back to your journal notes from the beginning about your cycle of life and the insights into each area and what might be tripping you up (that was Step 5 of the cycle of life exercise). Re-read the feedback from your respected friends or colleagues about your weakness and possible glitch, and take note of anything that resonated with you in the statements about the five glitches. Also be aware of the voice in your head that tells you how you cannot achieve your goals. They have been screaming at you since you started this book, haven't they?

Now look at your three goals so that we can shift the particular limiting beliefs that are standing in your way. Things do not just happen to us – we are active participants in our life (regardless whether it is good stuff or bad stuff), and when we realize that the beliefs we hold are determining our experiences, we can start doing something constructive to alter it.

Ask yourself these questions:
- What limiting beliefs could I be holding on to that are creating these patterns and ongoing negative experiences?
- As I look at my vision board and read my three goals, some of the negative voices and feelings that yell at me and tell me that I will not achieve them are…

and let yourself write, write, write.

You may also realize you have some biggies in other areas of your life. Just record them all. It can help to think about what your parents, teachers, significant adults, church elders, etc. said, did and taught you, or simply what you started believing in response to them.

For example, if your finances are one of your low areas and are sitting on 20%, ask yourself what limiting beliefs you hold around money, abundance, your ability with money, your ability to earn, keep or save money. You might get things like:
- I must get a good job, regardless of whether it makes me happy.
- I have no discipline when it comes to spending.
- I don't understand money.
- I have to buy people nice gifts so they will like me.
- The economy is bad so I can't go for a better salary.
- I have to wear trendy, expensive clothes so I am not laughed at.
- Money doesn't grow on trees.
- Women can't earn lots of money.
- Men should be the breadwinners.
- No one in my family knows how to make money.
- You have to work hard to get anywhere.

- Rich people are bad people.
- I can't do what I love and make money.
- Things are so expensive; there is no way I can save.

Do you get the picture? Your financial fire is not out because of anything anyone else did to you. It did not simply happen to you. You may not love hearing that right now, but your self-limiting beliefs are a huge factor in creating your reality. I did not promise that this course was going to be easy, but I did promise to help you to ditch your glitch, and that requires blatant honesty and taking responsibility.

Your beliefs are one of the keys to getting your life on track again. Spend some quality time finding all your beliefs that are in some way holding you back and messing with your life.

When you have done that, you should have a powerful list of self-limiting beliefs for the three areas. You may also wish to add any other big ones that you feel need to be there, no matter which area of life they fall under.

Some common examples that trip us up are:
- I'm stupid. I can't do anything right, so why try?
- No one supports me, so I will never get there.
- People always leave me.
- It's not okay to say no to people.
- I don't know how to manage my time.
- It's not safe to share my feelings.
- What I think is not important.
- I'm no good at sport, maths, business, relationships…
- I mustn't rock the boat.
- I'm not at all creative.
- There is never enough time.

Have some fun getting this list together. It can be very liberating to find your limiting beliefs and write them all down. Keep asking the question: "What limiting beliefs could I be holding on to that create negative results or experiences in my life?"

You can share your discoveries with the online community and be inspired by the other brave souls doing this work. The details are on page 22.

REMINDER

Remember to still to do the following every day:
- Light your candle to remind yourself that you are re-igniting your personal fire.
- Write in your gratitude journal. AIM for 12 things.
- Rate your personal fire and do something to stoke it.
- Refer to your action plan and vision board.

Here's to a fiery day!

CLIENT INSPIRATION

There came a time in my life where I had achieved so much and yet felt that I was just living aimlessly, going through the motions, completing the tasks for the day and collapsing into bed, only to start it all again the next day.

What was the point of it all? Where had I gone, where was the teenage girl that left high school and thought, "Watch out world, here I come"? Where was the young woman whose house was always filled with friends, laughter, love, music and dancing? Where was the woman who loved and cherished every moment of her day, even at work, and loved and cherished everyone around her? Where was the woman who believed in herself, the universe and the impossible, and who lived life to the fullest?

Where did I go, what happened? When did dreams, inspiration and fun get replaced with shopping, dishes, chemicals for the pool and endless traffic? When did I give up?

> *"Life's journey is not to arrive at the grave safely in a well-preserved body, but rather to skid in sideways, totally worn out, shouting 'Holy shit... what a ride!'"*
> Hunter S. Thompson

This realization triggered a depression for me. I began thinking that all was lost.

But I was missing the point. This was an opportunity, a chance to remember the depths of my being and get up. When life strikes you down, it is a chance to reinvent yourself, to become anyone you want. All you need is exceptional bravery to journey inwards and someone like Kate to guide you.

> *"You are your own worst enemy; unless you conquer yourself little else can be done."*
> Unknown

My dear friend C.V, to whom I owe so much, introduced me to Kate and I chose to do the Ignite your Life course. The course is a real soul search and I had to face aspects of myself that I didn't want to. It was difficult.

Kate's course took me through goals, actions, responsibility, fears, emotional baggage and boundaries.

The most difficult task in the course for me was limiting beliefs. I realized that most of what I do in life and the pressure that I put on myself is to combat the belief that I am unworthy of love. I need to be an exceptional achiever and perfect to be worthy of love. I remember spending nights crying through this course, because I'd seen the unconscious beliefs that were driving my life. The miracle is that only what comes into the light and is understood can be dealt with.

Kate taught me that a small shift every day in the right direction would eventually add up and change your life. I firmly believe that you should try everything. Maybe 95% of what you try will not make a difference or will be a total failure, but the last 5% will change your life.

Kate's course has something for everyone; you will find the 5% needed to change your life in the reading and exercises and you will be eternally grateful. Kate makes you face yourself, your values, beliefs and fears and ingeniously shows you how to change it all. I found myself on this course, I found a woman who no longer belittles herself, and for the first time believes that she is worth something and is not afraid to be herself. I love the life that I have started building around the way that I would like it to be, and Kate taught me how. Kate, I am so thankful and grateful for you and your course. You were the 5% (and more) that I needed.

Colette Delezenne

STEP 11:
Limit your self-limiting beliefs

Be mindful of your beliefs; they frame your feelings
Be mindful of your feelings; they frame your thoughts
Be mindful of your thoughts; they frame your actions
Be mindful of your actions; they frame your life
Be mindful of your life; it frames the universe
Kate Emmerson

My story

I was first exposed to the idea of limiting beliefs while studying coaching (my psychology education had never addressed this stuff) and did this exercise 12 years ago. It gave my inner flame a wee glimmer of hope. I had used some affirmations for healing in my 20s through the Louise Hay work, but this time around it was a layer deeper for me. I suddenly knew that these beliefs were re-enforcing my real glitch. They were the chief culprits that kept me stuck in endless loops of helplessness; they were throwing water on my personal fire. Until we actually go looking for these pesky saboteurs or glitches, we mostly just operate on autopilot, bemoaning our life but not understanding that we are the ones creating it. I was both astounded and relieved to face that nagging voice in my head and putting it all down on paper.

Those beliefs immediately seemed less scary. They were there, but a tad more under my control. They felt better on paper where I could face them, as opposed to in my head, running my life so negatively. It made me feel better to actively seek them out, be honest and brave enough to acknowledge them and write them down. Now that I had uncovered them, there was something I could take control of and start doing. There was less blaming other people. I really did feel a sense of relief.

The very next question that popped up was, "Okay, so now what?" It is one thing to find self-limiting beliefs, but unless you can shift them, they can still wreak havoc.

I had to face up to the beliefs I was carrying around. Some of them were pretty mean:
- I'm not good enough to be loved. (Remember the partner who cheated on me?)
- Am I a good enough life coach to start this business?
- Can I cut it in a new city? Especially a big one like Johannesburg?
- What if this business fails?
- I'm a failure. I'm no good at business.
- I'm not good with finances.
- Women in my family aren't able to make money.
- I can't stick to anything.

After two years of working and traveling abroad, I came back to South Africa to see my family and friends. It was supposed to be a quick visit before I gallivanted up Africa, doing HIV/Aids volunteer work, but then my mum asked me to join her business. I agonized over that decision for four days before deciding to stay.

It was the very best and the very worst decision of my life. Have you ever had any of those? And that is such a self-judgment, isn't it? It was just a decision that I made at the time.

I knew it was an opportunity to prove that I had what it takes, that I support my family, that I was an entrepreneur and so much more. I was offered shares in the business, which was a huge bunch of carrots for potential growth, but in all honesty I just battled my way through, doing the best I could at the time. It was a steep learning curve. My dad was the most incredible entrepreneur, and I knew I had his capacity and head for business. (Fast forward 25 years and I finally feel like I am owning that capacity 200%.) But boy, oh boy, some things take time. Not all glitches are as easy to shift as others.

It's the journey of life that forces us to blossom and grow. I had the most amazing support team of like-minded friends who kept me going and helped me do self-awareness work. I also I got involved with one of my passions – I did my first aromatherapy course and just fell in love with the modality of massage and those beautiful fragrant oils. I eventually studied a professional accredited course in massage, aromatherapy and reflexology and these modalities became part of my professional life.

Meanwhile, the business side of things with my mum and dad was growth inducing. I learned how much stamina I naturally had. I realized not everyone is meant to own a business. I realized how much I loved clients and how good I was with them. I learned about boundaries. But my mum and I never enjoyed the financial fruits of our very hard labor. It was particularly challenging, and it is testimony to our closeness that we managed to remain friends and not kill each other.

I also remember having to fire a staff member who was more than double my age. She was training our competition. I felt sick to my stomach but it was a quick lesson in taking instant control. I never forget asking her to meet me for coffee before her shift started and having to confront her about it. I was furious with her, and then relieved when she was finally out of the business. Clutter to be let go of!

The time eventually came to try to sell the business as the losses were just not worth it. I had already successfully relocated the business to halve our crippling expenses, and still we were not cutting it. Mum, Dad and I set a date and decided to call it quits. At the last minute this was reneged on and, to my sheer amazement, I decided to leave anyway and go overseas again. I felt like I was betraying them both, running away and leaving my mum lumbered with this "baby", but I needed to get a life of my own. I was suffocating and losing all sense of self-confidence.

And yet in less than a year I came back. My dad had managed to pay off a huge part of the loan, and said I could give it one more shot. I never knew the 80/20 rule back then, that 80% of the results come from 20% of the resources. I was playing with the wrong part of the business, focusing all my energy on the 80% and not the 20%. What the hell was I thinking? By then I was a professional aromatherapist. I was able to employ Mum and pay her a bit for her time, and we managed to limp on for a while longer, before eventually selling up via a business broker, at a very small price, just to get rid of the business.

It was a painful time. I remember my dad yelling at me with his face just three inches from mine, and later over the phone, about how useless I was and that I always made the wrong financial decisions and would never amount to anything. "You are a failure," he yelled.

You can imagine it got even worse the next year when I told my family that I was sexually interested in women. My dad didn't speak to me for a year, such was the level of his judgment against me. It robbed me of my self-confidence at so many levels. Even sharing this story with you now brings back all those memories to me – the pain, the hurt, the loss, the lack of belief in my potential and capability.

Fifteen years later, in 2010, I found myself doing more personal development work on my finances, reading Suze Orman's book *The 9 Steps to Financial Freedom*. There were deep, difficult challenges to write about, and for the first time I realized something massive in my life. With a fat slap, I woke up to the devastating fact that I was carrying around the guilt, shame and embarrassment of that time in my 20s, and had manifested the exact same amount of financial debt in my personal life as the amount of money the business had lost so many years ago. That correlation coming to light was one of the most profound insights of my life.

Our glitches can run deep and long, make no mistake – but, dear reader, at some point you will find yourself naturally compelled to find the pieces of your puzzle, no matter how much pain and heartache you have to go through to see it all.

There are still times when I feel like I carry the last remnants of that time, just as with the bulimia, so I am always vigilant and conscious about my own personal glitches. This work we embark on is not some magic pill. Untangling patterns of sabotage takes some hard, honest work. And yet the journey to the other side, to freedom, is always worth it. Our life calls us to become more, to expand and to grow, to be who we are destined to be.

I now surrounded myself with the most amazing people who believe in the highest version of me. They keep me on the straight and narrow and help me to push myself, especially when I am ready to give up on myself and an old glitch is rearing its familiar head. I do the same for them. It's called support AND masterminding.

CLIENT INSPIRATION

We were given planks that we were going to break. On one side we had to write what we were doing habitually that was holding us back and on the other, we had to write our desired outcome after breaking those shackles and reaching our highest potential.

I wrote "enabler" on my negative side and "spiritual growth" on my positive side. I was so confident that I'd get good results. I was so strong. I was going to whack this plank and smash it! What a joke. When my turn came, I hit that bloomin' plank with all my might, and nothing! I tried again. Still nothing. I was so defeated. I thought I was so strong.

What I later learned from this is that I'd been fooling myself that I'm strong when in actual fact I'm a total slave to being controlled by those around me. I was emotionally manipulated. I might be an enabler but I was absolutely not in control of my own life. I realized how I've allowed myself to be played over the years. I became so angry, picked up my plank and smashed in across my knee. It split in two. I felt a sense of satisfaction and relief. It was an absolute breakthrough.

It has taken almost a year to be free of this condition. I'm finally aware when I'm being played. I can stand back and do nothing, not allow myself to be played and not feel guilty.

I now put my needs before those of others. I've grown spiritually and feel almost whole again. I can say without a doubt that I no longer enable people. My eyes are open and spiritually I'm more aware.

I can only say thanks to Kate for her insight and always knowing which buttons to push.

Granny Bev

LET'S GET SHIFTING

Today we're going to do an easy seven-part process to shift these beliefs around. I was introduced to some of the following steps in Jack Canfield's *The Success Principles*, and over the years have adapted it several times.

Find the biggest culprits

For each of the three areas of life you have goals in, pick two limiting beliefs that you found, so six beliefs in total. Choose the ones that you know have the biggest negative impact on you; they will be triggering some of the other ones, and so they are the most powerful ones to start with. There are always one or two that we know are more destructive than the others or that run through every facet of life. So, my challenge to you is that you go for the biggest culprits, as shifting them will have the most positive and significant impact.

Now choose just one to start with as we go through the rest of the exercise. You will come back and repeat this process with each of them. Write the belief out again at the top of a new page, perhaps in your journal. For example, "My negative limiting belief is that I do not know how to make more money."

LOOK FOR THE SOURCE

Spend some time wandering back in your life, looking at where this belief came from. You might write, "I grew up in a family that always accepted low-paying jobs for hard work. We never had enough. I was told at school that it's good to settle for whatever job you can get, so long as you have a job. Anyway, I don't have a degree."

Debunk it

What evidence do you have to support that this belief is false? Are there any ideas, people, friends, experiences from your own life or famous people that will prove that perhaps this is not true for everyone? Can you think of any real-life examples when a statement like this was not true?

For example: "I have a friend at school who grew up poorer than us who but has a million-dollar company now. In my 20s I was very good at finding extra ways to pay for trips. In emergencies I have always managed to come up with extra money."

How does this keep you stuck?

The next step is to determine how holding onto this belief is messing with your life and keeping you stuck. Our beliefs cause us to feel, then think, then act or behave in a certain way that proves this limiting belief to you. So, keeping the same example as above:

The way this belief is messing with me is that I…
- Feel completely stuck in this low-paying job.
- Am in debt and don't know how to get out of it.
- Feel trapped, useless and pathetic.
- Can't see a brighter future for myself.
- Feel there is just no hope.
- Can't plan for a holiday that I want.

Look for a better alternative

What do you want to manifest instead of this? What you would rather be thinking, feeling, doing and acting on to positively ignite your life? Using the same example…

I'd prefer to live with the following:
- I have choices in my life.
- I can learn how to make more money.
- The future can be brighter.
- I have control over being able to pay off my debt.
- I can go on holiday to somewhere special.
- I can learn how to make more money than I am currently earning.
- I have possibility in my life.

Choose a new affirmation

Can you see that the original limiting belief creates everything that's keeping you stuck?

If you truly want what you wrote in the previous step, then you can't have your self-limiting beliefs. They are incompatible. What you have in your life will show you what you believe about your life. If you want something different to what you have, not only do you have to take a different action and do all the other steps in this book, but you also need to get to the root cause and treat that.

What is the new affirmation or statement that you can start imprinting on your subconscious brain?

TIP: Rather than vehemently trying to state the exact opposite of your limiting belief, try something a bit more realistic, gentle and powerful that creates a pathway or movement towards a new, empowering, positive belief.

If you start yelling from the rooftops, "I can make as much money as I want" or "I'm a billionaire"– well yes that's possible, but chances are high that your fear, lack of self-belief and natural distrust will kick in. You will be back to nursing your old belief in a heartbeat.

I prefer to include a "process" word in your new statement of belief that gets you started in the direction in which you wish to proceed.

Which of these powerful process words do you love?
- opening
- becoming
- activating
- increasing
- manifesting
- calling in
- accelerating
- awakening
- expanding
- emerging
- growing
- willing
- creating

If your original belief is "I do not know how to make more money", you might want to try some of these new affirmations:
- It's possible for me to expand my ability to learn how to make more money.
- I can increase my knowledge of how to earn more money.
- I'm growing my money awareness and awakening ideas of how to make more money.
- I am activating new ideas through being willing to make more money.

Just experiment. When you have a new statement of possibility, it will gently nudge you along towards where you wish to go, helping to support your goals in life.

Find a way to make it happen
Now that you have your new statement of possibility, the last step is to ask yourself the following: "As I hold this new belief as possible, what do I need to do that will support and strengthen it?"

Using the same example from above, you might write:

I could…
- Ask my friend John, who runs his own business, for help.
- Speak to my boss about a raise.
- Chat to HR about courses I can attend through work to increase my skills.
- Join a networking group and chat to people who are already making more money.
- Ask someone to mentor me.
- Find a community business center and learn from the people there.
- Find a book by someone who knows this stuff.
- Get personal coaching.

- Chat to people online.

When you have created this list, please add these new action steps that will support this new possibility to your structured action plan.

Now go back to the beginning and do the same process with your next limiting belief. Take the time to complete the process for all six beliefs. I promise that you will feel so much more in control of yourself and your inner flame after you've done so.

A CHALLENGE FOR YOU

Write your six wonderful, affirming new beliefs along with your top three goals. Remember you were asked to write your goals out on little cards and put them up everywhere? You can add your new positive beliefs to your daily action plan. They have got to be visible.

It's through the repetition that you will slowly start shifting the old patterns and replacing them with more empowering new ones. Every time you feel yourself reverting to your old beliefs, read through all your steps to re-enforce the new belief, and the old one will steadily get smaller. It takes patience, persistence and application. Your new beliefs will assist you to break through your self-sabotage so that you can achieve the goals you have created with grace and ease.

Read your goals along with your new positive beliefs at least every morning and night, before or after you look at your vision board. Can you see how you are creating a compelling destination as well as now being mindful of the roadblocks, obstacles and challenges along the way? Keep your beliefs with you as much as possible. The more you get them into your system, the better.

My story

I find that when I drive around my city in a space of deep and heartfelt gratitude, rather than stuck in my own headspace of self-limiting beliefs, that the world comes alive before my eyes. I see things that I don't notice otherwise, I connect better with my driving, I'm more in flow, and feel fueled by what I see.

Just this week I noticed an elderly lady on a bicycle, hair flowing wildly behind her, cycling on the side of the road. She was smiling from ear to ear. Then I noticed that running alongside her on the grassy verge, without a lead, was a beautiful big brown dog. His tongue was lolling out and he had a big grin on his face as he ran steadily, keeping pace with her. This was in the center of Johannesburg, which is considered to be a crime-ridden city, and here was this woman having a fabulous outing with her dog.

I know without a shadow of a doubt that when I am not in gratitude, I close off completely. I'm in a hurry to get home; I'm grumpy and stressed; I drive too fast; I play negative limiting beliefs such as, "Ugh Johannesburg is such a crazy city and so full of stress and crime..." I'm not connected to my world. But when I let go of that and stay in the present moment, I feel full of joy at what is around me.

LET ME KNOW

I'd love to hear about the affirmations you're using to let go of self-limiting beliefs. Please share them with our private Facebook group. If you haven't joined yet, the details are on page 22.

A LITTLE TASTE...

Before we finish up for today, here is a head's up for our next step. Please grab yourself a three kilo pack of big baking potatoes and a plastic bag that you can see through.

That's got you curious, hasn't it?

STEP 12:
Lug your load

"The weak can never forgive. Forgiveness is the attribute of the strong."
Mahatma Gandhi

I bet you have been wondering about my last request that you get some big potatoes and a clear plastic bag. Think about the fact that you might be able to braai (that's the South African version of a barbeque) those potatoes at the end of the exercise!

I love to keep you guessing.

If you didn't gather your potatoes, please do not keep reading as I know you will simply be deciding if you are going to do this exercise or not. Just trust and do it as this is a very powerful exercise that will shift your perception.

So you need a bag of potatoes (the nice big baking ones) and a large clear plastic bag.

CLIENT INSPIRATION

I felt like my life was in a total rut and I didn't even have the energy to get out of it. Kate had helped me change my life previously, so when she suggested her Ignite Your Life course, I was really keen and believed it was just the thing I needed for the change I desperately longed for.

The course was intense, challenging and totally ignited my life. At the same time it was manageable and I felt very supported. What I really loved about it was my time to journal, which let my new learnings and epiphanies sink in and take root.

The potato exercise was definitely my favorite part (although maybe not at the time!), as it had the biggest impact on my life and helped me sort out so many things that were keeping me stuck in my big fat rut. It was so freeing! The exercise of dealing with the "potatoes" was really helpful, especially as I wasn't used to having conversations like that. It gave me the blueprint to tackle these situations and to this day, I regularly look at this exercise and if need be, deal with situations that have arisen.

I'm so grateful for this course and the ignition and freedom I gained from it!

Carol-Ann Milne

Please make sure you have made contact with me via the private Facebook group. The contact details are on page 22. You do not need to be doing this journey alone, so make time to come and post stuff and share how you are coping and what is positively shifting for you. It is important to me. We can all benefit from additional help, so please don't struggle along on your own. These journeys are not always easy to engage in, and it is a sign of strength to ask for support. I look forward to hearing from you, whether it's to celebrate your shifts or find new solutions to help you along the path to achieving your goals.

This exercise is about finding all the harsh things that people have done to you that have in some way negatively affected you, dampened your personal fire, or made you so angry you could have started a fire with all the heat in your belly. The first thing you need to do is grab your journal as you'll be writing in it. Light your candle, take a deep breath and let's go, step by step.

WHO DID WHAT? WHO SAID WHAT?

Take some time to wander back through your life and look for the types of people detailed below. They can be dead or alive, in the same country as you or not. It doesn't matter. You may not even know where they live right now. Write down their names, and next to that, the date when it – whatever it is – took place (the year is good if you can remember), or perhaps the age you were when it happened. Do not despair if you have no date or age but you just recall the event and the feelings it elicited in you.

If you're wondering if someone is significant or not, the simple test is this: if you saw that person in front of you today, would you have all sorts of crazy, angry, hurt immediate reactions in your head, heart and body? If you answer yes, then there is unfinished business and you should write down their name.

We're going to start by looking for the people, no matter who they are to you now or who they were to you, who you have never been able to forgive 100% for something that they did to you. It doesn't matter what they did, but you know in your heart if you have not forgiven them and are holding on to that in some way. Write down the date and the event that happened. If there were a few of them, write down the dates of as many as you can remember.

Next, look for all the people that you feel some kind of jealousy, possessiveness or envy towards, along with the dates you can remember of any incidents that seem relevant.

Then look for people who betrayed you and your kindness or trust in some way so that you are still feeling the pain of that betrayal and hurt. Write about what it subsequently unleashed in your life.

Next make a list of all the people who said mean or hurtful things to you and with whom you have never had a courageous conversation about those incidents. These are the people you really want to say something to.

Make a list of anyone who has in some way taken you for a ride or taken advantage of you.

And – while we are at it – often the person we are the maddest at about something is ourselves. This can be your current adult self, or your younger child self.

You might need to add something else to your list. Are you mad at or feeling betrayed by God (or whoever is appropriate for you in that context) or the universe in general? Or perhaps all men, or all women?

Write down the names of anyone you know you are giving your energy and power to.

DISH OUT THE POTATOES

Now that you have a list of names and dates, can you guess what is next?

Take a potato, and write the name of each person that you have listed, along with the date, on the potato. Then pop it in the clear bag. If you have 50 names, you have 50 potatoes. If you have 10 names, you have 10 potatoes.

If, for some reason, you found only one person throughout this exercise (it has never happened yet), but this person is a "biggie" in your life, such as a parent, sibling, child or partner, find all the different aspects of that person that negatively affected you in some way, and give a potato and date to every incident. This is important if it is a particularly painful relationship.

Your challenge is to lug this load of potatoes around with you for the next week, which is until you get to step 16. Do you think I'm joking? Everywhere you go, your bag of potatoes goes with you. You keep it next to your bed at night; you take it to the toilet with you; you take it to work and wherever else you go. The only place you probably should not take it is into a supermarket as they might think you've shoplifted it.

Do not think that just writing down the names will be enough. The challenge and real gift is in doing this exercise properly. Yes, you will get funny looks, yes, you will get strange questions, yes, you will get tired of it, and yes, you may even forget it in places. You have to look after this bag for the next week.

I know there will be several reasons why you really feel you cannot do this: you are too busy, you can't take it to work, what will people think? What a silly exercise, Kate... None of these excuses are actually valid. I mean that. None of them are valid. So, you have a funky new partner in the form of a bag of potatoes for the next week. I don't care how much you dislike me in this moment. If you found a name for a potato, you gotta lug it around!

CLIENT INSPIRATION

One morning on the retreat we had to isolate ourselves and write letters to our inner child and offer forgiveness. I remember sitting at the water's edge on a rock, writing and crying. I couldn't stop the tears, nor did I try.

That letter clarified letting go of years of sexual abuse and hatred, both for the perpetrators and myself – the loathing I felt for letting it happen to me. I realized I was the innocent one and I actually forgave myself.

It was so liberating. Forgiveness frees us from purgatory in real life. Hating someone for things of the past is a bit like drinking poison and expecting it to poison the one you hate. It's a useless attitude.

Granny Bev

A LITTLE REMINDER

You are still meant to be doing your daily exercises, so:
- Light your candle.
- Write in your gratitude journal.
- Rate your personal fire and take action to increase it.
- Take action on all your other commitments according to your personal goals and structured plan.
- Read your goals and new enriching beliefs.

Let's pause

"When we fail to set boundaries and hold people accountable, we feel used and mistreated. This is why we sometimes attack who they are, which is far more hurtful than addressing a behavior or a choice."
Brené Brown

Before we move on to the next step, let's evaluate our progress.

I am not sure how long you have been taking between each step laid out for you, but it has been a while since you created your first action plan in line with your goals. How is that working out for you so far?

Be really honest with yourself as you answer. I know it is easy to commit at the beginning, but to follow up every day, taking all the little actions in line with your goal, takes the strength of a Bengal tiger. In the Bikram yoga I do, there is one exercise called "awkward" that has people huffing, puffing and seriously digging deep into themselves. The teacher always talks about cultivating strength like a Bengal tiger. I sometimes growl softly under my breath as it helps me to visualize that strength. Be that tiger!

Maybe you're at the point in your schedule where tomorrow you will be enjoying some rewards for all you have achieved in the past week. Or perhaps you have let some of your actions and goals fall by the way side.

SUPPORT AND ACCOUNTABILITY

Always remember the online community is there to give you additional help. When my clients are doing the Ignite Your Life online program, those who are brave enough to check in regularly, share status updates and progress, admit they are battling, and ask for help and encouragement are the ones who find a way through the tougher stuff with more grace and ease.

I know it may not feel comfortable to divulge your personal stuff, but this community is a safe haven. The details are on page 22.

DO AS MUCH AS YOU CAN

As you create your next action plan for the week ahead, you will see a slightly different plan where you can now write your transformational beliefs on the same sheet. All these little steps build on each other, layer upon layer.

If all of this is still relatively new to you: please understand that it is entirely normal and reasonable not to get around to every single thing thrown at you. I do ask, however, that you are willing to look at every exercise and challenge, and do as much as you possibly can. Be honest with yourself about why you are not doing everything.

Do you need to improve your self-discipline and commitment this week? Be gentle yet firm with yourself as you take these steps forward. Just moaning that you are too busy and don't have enough time for the course will not cut it. Rather stop reading until you are ready to do the work required. No matter how busy your life is, this is about prioritizing things that matter so that you achieve the shifts you want to. This is about committing to changing your life, and the willingness to make yourself a priority. Re-read the commitment form you signed at the very beginning to strengthen your resilience.

LOOK BACK

Journal about how far you have come in the past week, how you feel you have done with your plan, reading your goals and new positive beliefs every day, lugging your potatoes around and all the other challenges I've thrown at you.

How are you feeling about the steps you have taken up to this point?
- Elated or down in the dumps?
- Pleased with yourself or irritated?
- Like you're progressing or stagnating?
- Enthusiastic or disillusioned?
- Excited about what's next or overwhelmed?
- Or something that is a mixture of all the above?

All of these are just emotions. You can either let them get the better of you and rule your life or you can choose to change them.

Round about now your glitch might be kicking in with all its power. It's normal. Embrace it as it's letting itself be known, but this time around be more conscious of it and the havoc it can wreak in your life.

RATE YOURSELF

Think about how much of your action plan you have achieved this week.

If you have completed 90 to 100% of all your actions in line with your goals for the month and are enjoying your rewards, very well done! You get a gold star.

If you have completed 50 to 90% of your actions for the week, what a cool start! Pat yourself on the back and acknowledge what has shifted. Then ask what happened, without blame, to the other ones that were on your action list. Can anyone else do them for you? I doubt it as this is about self-changes. Be honest with yourself and take responsibility. No excuses. But don't make yourself feel bad. More importantly, how can you take different action or get help so that you are in control of improving your output this week? Do you need to drop me a line?

If you noticed that you completed less than 50% of your self-allotted tasks and actions in line with your goals, stop and truly acknowledge what you have done this week, no matter how small the action. Well done for that. It is a step in the right direction, and there is no point in beating yourself up in any way whatsoever. Think about what happened this week. Did you take on too much, or were you unrealistic about what you could accomplish in your first week? Did you simply not pay enough mindful attention to it all and expect it to happen by itself? Or are old habits and beliefs getting the better of you?

If it wasn't poor planning, are you sure you even want these shifts? Take a few minutes to re-look your goals and see if you really want to achieve them. Without blame, feeling bad or any of those other useless emotions, just acknowledge what needs to shift this week to get you a little further along the path. Is it re-committing, taking a few actions off the list so you can get stuck in with the remaining ones, or do you need some extra support from a friend?

No matter which category you fell into this week, take a moment to breathe. Then you need to take total responsibility for how you are feeling at this point and then do something to improve it a little bit.

STEP 13:

Set ballsy boundaries

> *"'No' is a complete sentence."*
> Anne Lamott

Can you try this one thing in the next 24 hours? Just once, use the word "NO", with nothing else attached to it.

"No". Full stop.

While we all have a deep connection to the rest of humanity and have a shared planetary space that we live and breathe in that connects every single one of us, at the same time we each occupy our own unique space. Boundaries, or personal space, can be quite literal, encompassing the physical space directly around us that we feel comfortable in. In esoteric terms, this is our aura or bubble of energy. You know when someone gets too close to you and they feel as if they are "in your space"? That's your personal bubble of energy.

But having healthy boundaries is also figurative and less tangible, which can make them a bit harder to define. It is about knowing what you will and won't do, what you will and won't put up with, and how to prioritize your goals and actions and not let them be sabotaged by other people's agendas.

A WIN-WIN SITUATION

Having healthy boundaries means being willing to make yourself a priority, without making others feel pushed aside. And if they did feel pushed aside, that is actually their stuff to deal with, not yours. When you do not have healthy boundaries you can make everything that someone else does or doesn't do all about you.

Healthy boundaries create win-win situations. They are formed from having constructive, adult, rational conversations with yourself and others about what is and isn't important to you, and for all the right reasons.

Maybe you have been a pushover and people have taken you for granted. When you set ballsy boundaries, both you and those around you will have to adjust to the new situation. It can be hard to make the initial shift and start creating new definitions of what you will and won't put up with and what is acceptable and desirable to you.

People around you will be quite attached to your old ways of doing things, and perhaps even thrive on them. But healthy boundaries have no place for guilt, feeling bad or playing small.

YOU ARE IN CONTROL

Let's be blunt here: Your personal life was in need of some quick shifting, glitch ditching, and igniting, which is why you decided to read this book and do the exercises. But no one else actually "made" your life that way, or did it to you. While it may seem like other people have dampened your inner flame – or dowsed it completely with ice-cold water – the real insight is that you allowed it to happen, and until you take full responsibility for that, not much else will change. That may be a hard one to hear, and this always makes for an interesting discussion but sit with it for a bit.

Someone can only do something to you, as an adult, with your permission. No one else can control your thoughts unless you allow them. So if you let a friend take advantage of you, you did that. If your partner hits you, you let them. I am not saying that you made them hit you; I am saying that by staying in the relationship or staying in the house, then at some level you allow it to continue. You are accepting it and you actually can make different choices by leaving. It's not easy, but it's always possible.

You are always, always, always in control of your responses to whatever is happening around you in any given moment. You are most in control with the boundaries you have with yourself.

Choice and free will are some of the things that set humans apart from all other creatures. This is where your power lies. It can be a hard pill to swallow. I am not here to say what is right or wrong, but to tell you this: if you are able to contemplate the idea that people can only do to you what you allow them to, then you have a place from which to start changing your life once and for all.

Can you also start to see the inextricable link between your boundaries and your glitch? Lack of clear boundaries always leaves you worse off. Remember once again that you got your life to the point it was at a couple of weeks ago. It did not happen overnight, did it? I am not saying that bad, difficult or extremely challenging things have not come across your path and been thrown at you, but you are in control of your thoughts, time, intentions, energy, habits, choices and money. That is about it.

When you have positive, healthy and self-full thoughts, you have healthy boundaries and clearer relationships. If you are not in control of your mind and thoughts, then you let others dictate your life to you. If you are not living your life in a way that matters, who's to blame?

I will venture a guess and say a large contributor to your lack of inner flame and power is ill-formed boundaries, and not having the gumption or know-how to stand up for yourself and put your needs on the table. Recognize this? No matter where or how this shows up, when your fire is out, it can be traced to taking care of everyone else's needs but your own.

> "Be aflame with enthusiasm and people will come
> for miles around to watch you burn."
> John Wesley

WHAT DO WEAK BOUNDARIES LOOK LIKE?

So, how do you know when you do not have clear boundaries? Here are some telltale signs:

- You feel that others take advantage of you.
- You never feel truly heard.
- No one takes you seriously.
- People are often late for your meetings, whether they are social or professional.
- People often let you down.
- Others are usually promoted above you.
- Your opinion does not matter when you share it.
- You do not feel supported but always support others.
- You always try to help others get on the right track but seldom look at your life truthfully.
- You feel resentful towards people.
- You are often irritated with friends or colleagues for the things they "do to you" and how they treat you.
- When someone asks you to do something you will always try to do it, even putting off your own tasks.
- You don't speak up in a restaurant if something is wrong with your order.
- You will accept bad service and just complain afterwards to your friends.
- When your friend calls at 10 p.m. you always answer the phone, even though you go to bed at 9.30 p.m.
- You never take an afternoon nap or make time for yourself to do whatever you please.
- You feel your parents or kids take advantage of your time, money and energy.
- You often complain about things.

I could go on and on here. A lack of clear boundaries will leave you in last place, time and time again.

LET'S GET SHIFTING

For you to achieve the goals that you created at the outset, you will definitely need to re-look your boundaries. You cannot do one without the other. You will need to keep affirming what you want and that you are going to get it, no matter what you have to do (provided of course you do not consciously or intentionally hurt others along the way).

When boundaries are not in place, you can bet your bottom dollar that you will find excuse after excuse to do something that is not a priority, or put someone else's needs first. There is a time and place to support others, but remember that clear, healthy boundaries create amazing relationships, giving you the space to be self-full as well as allowing you to assist others.

So now I have got you thinking about healthy boundaries, what is the exercise to improve them practically? The challenge is quite simple:

- Start saying "yes" to yourself.
- Start saying "no" to others.

But how? It sounds so simple but can be really hard to implement, so try this for the duration of this work. (But please use your common sense. If your boss asks you to do something that is part of your role at work, you are not going to use the following method, okay?)

You press pause. From now on, when someone asks you to do something, to go somewhere, to make something happen, to call someone, whatever it is, you are going to create a pause. It can sometimes help to have one standard answer to fall back on. You might want to try some of the following:

- Let me check my diary and see if I can make it.
- Let me think about it and come back to you.
- I need to talk to XYZ and find out if this is possible.
- Can I please give you an answer tomorrow?
- Please come back in 15 minutes and I will give you my answer.
- I am very busy with this project deadline right now, so please can we chat about this at 5 p.m?

While these may not cover every single example of where you need to reclaim yourself, it is a great way to start exercising your ballsy boundary muscles. Do whatever it takes so that you do not instantly say "yes" to others or "no" to yourself.

From now on, simply create a small gap between the input and your response. In that gap, re-evaluate your own goals and priorities and see if the request correlates in a positive way with what you want. When you give yourself this space, you are reclaiming your power.

The first time you say "NO" to someone will be the hardest. Do it anyway.

My story

One of my favorite things is to meet people from all over the world. I get such a buzz from it. It can be a once-off fleeting moment or a meaningful ongoing relationship. So you can image what it is like for me right now as I am finishing this book. I've made it my highest priority, with a few other big projects just behind it. I get requests for meetings, coffee chats and potential client opportunities. And then there's meeting up with the delightful souls in my life. My standard response is: "I'd love to meet with you and I am only free after mid-April." I've even done this for big events I'm speaking at. Yikes, it's hard!

It is about choice in every moment. Sitting at my desk for hours on end, day after day, can get tiring, tough, lonely, and sometimes even a tad boring when my bum is numb. "Ooh, wouldn't getting out be lovely?" I think and start letting my concentration and focal point wander. So I get up, do some exercise, grab water and a snack, and come back to write.

To keep all these amazing balls successfully and mindfully in the air and stay at my personal peak, I have to be vigilant, ruthless and quite candid about my time and energy. People say, "Can't we just have a quick 10 minute call?" Well, no, actually, because that is going to take up mental and emotional space. I have to focus on my number-one priority. It's such a lesson in self-worth and valuing my own priorities rather than someone else's.

REMEMBER YOUR GOALS

You need to be willing to be honest with your responses and say "no" when necessary, "yes" when you need to, or re-negotiate something half way. Give yourself the opportunity to change your habits one bit at a time.

For example, if you have a health and fitness goal for the month and your friend invites you to tea at a coffee shop where you know there is going to be a huge decadent chocolate cake, you may want to think about that. If you know you always say "yes" to cake at that shop and then feel bad afterwards, why not this time say you will check your diary as you have a busy week?

In the "pause" time, ask yourself what will happen at the end of your time period if you have not reached your goal? Will you be disappointed? Mad? Does this request require a little bit of negotiating rather than an outright no? What if you were to say "I'd love to come to tea and catch up with you but can we go to a different place this time? There's a café where they make amazing energy smoothies everyone is talking about. I am on a health kick and don't want to tempt myself by seeing that gooey cake again." Isn't this a fair request? What is the worst that can happen? They can say "no" and then you will have to determine if you want to go and eat the cake, or go and not eat the cake. Maybe you can eat the cake and revel in it, and do something different tomorrow to get back on track to reach your goal.

Or perhaps you have a goal to create two extra hours every week to complete certain things required for your new business to secure that big project you want. But you spend time in traffic because you always travel to visit your friend on the other side of town. This time when she asks you to come and visit, pause and reflect on the value of losing that time in traffic, and what could happen if you spent it on your business instead. If you are at a critical point and have not yet created your two hours this week, perhaps you could ask her to come and visit you. Or meet half way.

Doing this work is about making new, conscious choices in the moment rather than operating in your default, habitual mode.

Creating healthy new boundaries requires a depth of honesty that can seem hard at the beginning. It gets easier each time. You need to trust yourself, remember what is important to you, and honor yourself and the time you are making for your life. Don't let others' demands pull you off course.

There is a place on the latest action plan for you to make a note of the healthy boundaries you have been creating. I know you can do this. Let me know how you are putting healthy boundaries in place on our Facebook group. If you haven't joined yet, the details are on page 22.

STEP 14:

Live your values

"A true balance between work and life comes with knowing that your life activities are integrated, not separated."
Michael Thomas Sunnarborg

Dare I ask how you are doing with lugging your bag of potatoes around? Have you still got them with you? Or have you stopped the exercise? There are still a couple of days to go and I am sure you are already getting some insights from the exercise.

OUR GUIDING LIGHTS

Today we are going to look at what values are all about. This is such a wonderful exercise to do, and while there are many ways to find your values, this one is super easy and simple. But before you peek ahead, I want to chat about what values are.

Values are essentially the ideals and principles that we use as we navigate our life, and they create the personal identity that shapes and defines us. You can even think of them as personal fingerprints, as you leave their trace over everything that you touch and do. They are unique to you.

Whether we consciously know what our values are or not, they will always guide what we do, what we say and whether we are deeply content or miserable. They are what motivate us.

Our values offer us our "why" in life. They tell us what we value in life. They guide our assumptions and beliefs. They are the reason why we want to do some things or experience certain ways of being.

Our inner driving force is underpinned by our personal values. When you know what yours are, then you can use them constructively in your life. If you do not know what they are, and if you are not living in line with your values, then the chances are high you are living according to someone else's values. Think about that... Not living in accordance with your values also means that you are constantly fighting yourself and what is important to you. That can lead to a life of despair.

All values are neutral in that no one particular value can be objectively "better" than another. It is just a question of which ones are more important to you. While all values are inherently positive and affirming, the beliefs and goals that we choose to build around our values can be life enhancing or life defeating.

For example, if courage is a top value to you, that is what you will yearn to be all the time. From your life experiences, you may have adopted the self-limiting belief that, "I will never be able to start my own company because I don't have a degree". Can you see how your value would desperately want you to start a business and reach for that goal, but the belief you have adopted will squash it every time? It is so important to know what your values are, so that they can guide your life path, guide your goals and give you the opportunity to weed out any limiting beliefs that are not enabling you to live according to your values.

"Every choice or decision you make is based on your values. Whenever you decide between alternatives, you invariably choose the alternative that you value the most. Because you can only do one thing at a time, everything you do is a demonstration of what you consider to be the most important at that moment. Therefore, organizing your values in an order of priority is the starting point of personal strategic planning."
Brian Tracy

HARNESS THEIR POWER

Today is about consciously recognizing your values, so that if your life is not yet congruent with them, you can start harnessing them and adapting your life around them. Often what happens is that we adapt our values around our life, and this always trips us up.

For real change, we need to start from the inside out, creating your life and your goals around your values. It means that you are able to bring more of yourself to the world and shine your light brightly. The world needs you to be YOU in your own unique way.

As values underpin and motivate everything, it makes sense to work with them rather than against them. When you ignore your values, or negotiate them in some way, you will feel the negative implications. There will be a sense of dread, unease, restlessness or discontent. When your inside does not match your outside, it causes chaos. You will feel like there is something out of kilter. Your glitch will be right there. Even if your inner fire is lit, working against your values is like throwing a little water on your fire every day, making it harder for it to burn.

You may also have to get over any fears and allow yourself to work towards fulfilling yourself rather than avoiding the things you fear. For example, you might fear rejection, yet have the value of expertise. You may know that you want to stand up and deliver a keynote presentation at an international congress, yet your fear of rejection could win. So would you ever chase after that goal? Chances are that you wouldn't. So often we will betray our values rather than face the fear, or unpack the limiting belief. What is the cost of that?

You are worth more than that.

Are you willing to walk towards your values, even if it means overcoming your obstacles along the way? Can you also see the link here between values, boundaries and self-limiting beliefs? Often we have to really learn to stand up for exactly what we want, by saying "yes" to ourselves and "no" to others.

TODAY'S EXERCISE

Now you can go ahead and complete the exercise. Give yourself some quiet time and space as this requires complete honesty – of course! Read through these values, and the instructions that follow.

VALUE	DESCRIPTION
Achievement	Accomplishing things that are important to you
Challenge	Stretching beyond your current comfort zone
Adventure	Real sense of joy, excitement and energy
Family	Genetic connection or other meaningful bonds
Friendship	Sharing and connecting with others
Independence	Relying on yourself and acting alone
Courage	Being bold, daring and saying "yes" to things
Leadership	Motivating, influencing and creating a vision for others
Integrity	Staying true to who you are and your beliefs. Being whole and aligned
Loyalty	Commitment to people or projects that overrides everything
Power	Control over decisions, resources and direction
Respect	Knowing others feel this towards you and you to others
Security	Stability, safety, structures in place for status quo
Contribution	Serving others, the community and environment. The legacy you leave
Marriage	Commitment to another person
Abundance	Flow of everything in and out, no scarcity
Intimacy	Very close, deep and potentially vulnerable connection
Freedom	Absolute choice and options about everything
Creativity	Expansive, out-of-the-box possibilities
Generosity	Sharing of self, time and resources to help others in need
Compassion	Heartfelt connection and understanding of fellow beings
Success	Attaining what you desire – feeling of making "it"
Acceptance	Willingness that everything is okay just the way it is
Vitality	High energy and health levels
Trust	Faith to rely on self, others and the universe ("God")
Expertise	Being on top of your game, best in your field and a reliable source of information
Love	Living from your heart and soul, seeing beauty in everything
Honesty	Seeing things as they are, without masks and speaking the truth
Knowledge	Continued understanding and acquiring of information
Passion	Deep sense of purpose, energy and fulfilment

Take out ten

The first thing is to eliminate 10 values from the above 30. Simply place a cross in the left-hand column of the 10 values that are not *that* important to you. Remember you are not necessarily talking about how you are currently living your life, but about what you know is important to you, deep inside your heart.

Lose another ten

Do the same again, eliminating another 10 values you are prepared to give up from the list by marking them with a cross.

It can take some time to do these first two parts of the exercise. It is normal to want to keep them all, but that is not the point of the exercise. While all these values are great and a wonderful way to live your life, it is impossible that all of them are vital to you. This is about priorities, as your values guide your life in every moment. So allow yourself to choose the ones that matter the most to you.

Another way of looking at this is to ask which values, if you could not honor them, would leave you feeling the most frustrated and unhappy (perhaps that is relevant in your life currently). These are the essential ones you have to keep.

Put them in order

Great, so now you are left with your top 10 values. The next step is to prioritize them, placing your highest value as number one, and then working down the list to number 10. For now, leave the right-hand column empty.

	TOP 10 VALUES	WHAT THEY MEAN TO ME
1		
2		
3		
4		
5		
6		
7		
8		
9		
10		

Find your definition

Now use the right-hand column above to really define and interpret for yourself what this value means to you. Five people may have chosen achievement as a value, but it will be represented differently for everyone. It could be anything such as:
- Getting a first in exams.
- Receiving an award for excellence in your field.
- Being the best parent.
- Learning five new skills every year.
- Going to a new country every year.
- Running your own business and keeping a positive cash flow.

It is whatever is important to you when you interpret your value.

For each of your 10 values, ask yourself, "What would it take for me to feel this value?"

Play with this until it feels right for you, then write your interpretations in the right-hand column or in your journal.

Look at your life

This is the great part. Once you have a much clearer idea of your values and what is important to you and how you live your life, you can start assessing whether all the things you are currently doing and pursuing in your life are aligned with your values. It is vital to adapt your life to your values, not the other way around.

Check your goals – your current top three short-term ones, and the long-term ones you are aiming towards. Will they bring you closer to fulfilling your values? If so, that is wonderful.

If not, how long do you feel you will be able to live like this? Six months? A year? Or will it take some major life tragedy or illness to jerk you back on track and force you to make the changes your heart longs for?

Go and look closely at your vision board. Are your values jumping off the page at you? Do you need to add some more pictures and words?

As you allow yourself to shift into alignment with your values, a lot of the pain, heartache, despondency and despair that you may currently feel will dissipate. You can only live up to your core values by taking some emotional risks and making the shifts. Consider what needs to shift for you to get back in alignment with who you really are.

Spend some time writing in your journal about how closely aligned your life is to your values. Then blow out your candle and enjoy the rest of your day.

> "Sooner or later, those who win are those who think they can."
> Richard Bach

CLIENT INSPIRATION

I was about to enter into a contract with an entrepreneur who was launching a new project. I had some doubts about his experience, but I thought he was a smart guy who was doing something interesting and he'd learn what he needed to. Everyone told me that it was a great opportunity, and I should take it, even though I wasn't sure about him.

The more I dealt with this man, the more uncomfortable I felt. I had a deep sense of unease, but I couldn't understand exactly why. His inexperience wasn't that big a deal. I knew he would pick things up fairly quickly. The more I thought about it, the more I wanted to run away. But I didn't because I thought I was overreacting, and others who were dealing with him didn't have the reservations that I did.

Working through my values showed me what the problem was. I value being esteemed professionally, and this man didn't. He seemed to be focused on his own success and didn't recognize the value of the contribution I was going to make to his project. When I understood that, I immediately knew what to do. I withdrew from the contract. It was so empowering for me to follow my values and honor what I need. Thank you, Kate, for helping me to understand them.
SD

TELL ME

What has it been like for you to find out your core values? Do you know what kind of shifts you need to make so you can live in alignment with your values? Share your insights and questions with the Facebook community. The details are on page 22.

STEP 15:

Take action

"Everything you want is out there waiting for you to ask. Everything you want also wants you. But you have to take action to get it."
Jules Renau

There is nothing new for this step and yet it is the one that makes all the difference in the end. I know that life is busy. I have already a lot thrown a lot at you and you are lugging your load of potatoes around (don't worry, we will deal with those in the next step).

Wanting, hoping, visualizing, writing out goals, and journaling your feelings are great, but they will never replace you getting off your butt to take action in line with your future.

Have you been doing your fire rating every day, and then doing one small thing to take it up an incremental notch? Can you up the ante on that? From now on, every day there has to be action.

"First you jump off the cliff and you build wings on the way down."
Ray Bradbury

My story

At the beginning of 2015 some like-minded friends and I spent the day together in a beautiful empowering space, creating our magnificent vision boards for the year. We each brought something to share to eat, and I had specifically chosen pastries from around the world as everyone was committing to traveling. One friend wanted to manifest a sailing holiday in Turkey, so I chose Turkish pastries filled with ricotta cheese – I had never even known about them until that morning. It was a little way to add intention to action. After the personal success of my 2014 vision board, I really wanted to up the ante.

That was Sunday 11 January 2015. On Monday, the next morning, I woke up feeling paralyzed, overwhelmed and once again like a rabbit in the headlights. You know the feeling, right? Another series of events was unfolding regarding this book that you are holding in your paws. When my publishers took this book on, they suggested a submission date at the end of March 2015, so that we could have the printing date we wanted. Knowing what was going to be on my plate at the beginning of the year, I asked them if I could bring the submission date forward, to the end of January 2015. It was my choice, and I was messing up!

On the Monday morning after creating my vision board, I got an email from the publisher saying my contract was ready, but just days before I had realized I was in over my head. I had to ask Metz Press if we could revert to their original March deadline. That was a hard mail to write!

The reply mail I received said they had just done my contract, and to fit with my personal timeline to have the book released in July, my submission date was 16 February. A month away! If I wanted to submit at the end of March, they were cool with that, but then the date of birth for *Ditch Your Glitch* would be pushed to August 2015.

I went into a deep hole on that Monday, and it was all of my own sweet making (when isn't it?). I had to re-evaluate my own commitment to my year. It just got worse and worse as the day went on.

The reason why I had asked for the early submission date was because I thought it would be interesting to release my book in winter in the southern hemisphere, as it is the right time to snuggle up under a blanket in front of the fire with a glass of wine or hot chocolate and do lots of personal introspection. I thought it would be a great way to introduce this book to the world. But I realized what an impossible task lay ahead of me.

DO ONE THING A DAY

At about 5 p.m. on that bleak Monday, my very insightful mastermind support partner messaged me to ask how I was doing. I replied that my energy was low, I was overwhelmed and it all felt like too much. How the hell was I going to manifest this power-packed vision board in 2015? He wisely suggested I read something he had just put in our mastermind Dropbox.

Feeling somewhat low and irritated – and somewhat willing to stay in my self-created hole – I trusted him enough to go and read what he had put up. It was one of those simplified, somewhat annoying life-coaching type of boosters. I had to laugh as it's the very kind of thing I dish out to my clients and friends when they need a lift or a different perspective. It was the kind of thing that you are reading in this book. Don't you love the irony of life?

There were 24 points, simply titled "Time Hacks". As I read them with tears in my eyes, I could feel a glimmer of hope coming back. I hauled myself up by my knickers and sat down to make a list.

I knew that massive things were on the horizon for me, so it was just the feeling of being overwhelmed I was dealing with. I decided to go back to the basics: do one thing a day in line with my big goals. I made a list, from Monday to Sunday, and terrified myself by putting the biggest things first, which meant that very same day I had a huge thing to achieve. I then gave myself one thing to do each day for the rest of the week and started.

I knew I needed to switch my online platform for email delivery, newsletters, CRM, and an integrated shopping cart, along with creating a brand-new website. About a year before I had heard about Infusionsoft and their integration process whereby they coach you as you cross to their new platform. It was what I wanted.

With the rand-dollar exchange rate, it was fairly pricey though. In that moment of creating my "Just do it, dammit" list, I thought come hell or high water I would commit to it even if I couldn't commit to it that day.

Remember, it was still that same fateful Monday, at about 6 p.m. I Skyped the man from Infusionsoft, whom I had spoken to the year before, and told him that I needed to look at their current prices to see how we could break the costing down. I also said, "I need you to know that I cannot pay for it today but I commit to coming back to you in a week." Phew! It was done.

Can you see how even though I couldn't press "play" and purchase the product that day, I could commit to doing it the following week, and then I knew I had to get creative to find the funds. It was my form of commitment and being accountable to him – I knew that somebody was waiting for me.

AN EPIPHANY

So Monday's task got a tick. I committed to something big every day, and on Tuesday it was to respond to my publisher with my final decision. I had wanted to sleep on it. I woke up on Tuesday and had an epiphany. I knew I needed to go back to the March deadline for my book. It was my ego that wanted me to stick to the 16 February deadline.

I also thought, "Well, if I can write a book in two and a half months, then I know I can inspire others to do the same with me." I had already been running mastermind groups for the past four years, but had never had one on a specific topic. Within an hour I had written to the publisher asking for the end of March deadline, and posted on Facebook saying, "I am contemplating running a mastermind group for people who want to write a book. Who's interested?" Well, I kid you not, I got 30 replies, and within a week had 11 people signed up to start. That also became an income generator for me so I knew I could cover my bills for the two months I needed to write.

As I am writing this, it's Sunday 15 March, and I have people in Johannesburg, Cape Town, London, Scotland, Cyprus, Greece and Dubai involved in this mastermind group, and they all have beautiful books flowing forth from them.

ACCOUNTABILITY

One of the most important factors in your success is having a person or community to whom you are accountable, that will not accept excuses from you. I committed to updating my personal mastermind Dropbox every single day to keep me on track. With only one big thing to do every day, I suddenly found I had energy for additional tasks as well, and so the year got off to an incredible start.

I don't pretend this stuff is easy at any level, but I do know that it works. Sometimes we have to unconditionally love ourselves into action and sometimes we have to give ourselves a fat slap. Sometimes a combination of the two is best. Work with your glitch to get over your glitch.

What do you need to do today to get back into action mode, to allow yourself to live up to your dreams and be the magnificent soul that you are? Every time you take action you are showing the universe that you are willing to be seen.

GET ACTIVE

Look at your goals and take action. Look at your action list and take action. Look at yourself in the mirror and remind yourself why you are doing this.

Action is the best way to enforce the powerful law of ATTRACTION. In fact, look at what is inherent in that wonderful word – ACTION and TRACTION. So keep taking action as the traction will be imminent.

Please share the action you are taking with the Facebook community. The details are on page 22.

CLIENT INSPIRATION

At the start of my journey, I knew something was preventing me from moving forward. I felt stuck, but it was not a bad place. I had a secure job, great friends and family who were all supportive and loving, but I just could not move towards feeling more fulfilled and purposeful. I wanted to define and understand this block, which at that stage I could only refer to as "it".

I attended the Ignite Your Life course with Kate and four other wonderful souls to define and understand my block, with the hope of taking steps to overcome it. The work did not answer my questions (so I thought), but I enjoyed it as it took my focus away from those limits in my life. I thought that taking stock of my cycle of life and setting new goals would keep me busy while I looked for "it" and the way around or through "it". I kept my focus and energy on achieving the goals I set on the course and tried to maintain a conscious balance between mind, body and soul.

After a few weeks on this journey, I realized that the block was not one thing but that I was merely stuck in a complete comfort zone. What I thought was good and safe was actually my block. Looking at where I was and where I wanted to be, and taking small steps towards achieving those goals got me over this it. I discovered it is the practical, real-life actions and considerations that break down our self-imposed boundaries in life.

W Marcus

STEP 16:
Forgive and be free

> *"The truth is, unless you let go, unless you forgive yourself, unless you forgive the situation, unless you realize that the situation is over, you cannot move forward."*
> Steve Maraboli

Today is the day you can stop lugging your load of potatoes around. At last!

It is quite normal to feel a little emotional, tense or apprehensive doing this exercise.

Or a lot. It's important to remember that this is about letting go of the way you thought the past should be, to make peace with what happened and finally free yourself from the shackles of pain, hurt and resentment.

Letting go and surrendering allows you to be more present, engaged and enlightened. You are doing this for you, your life, your heart, your sense of self-worth and your freedom.

This potato exercise was inspired by a story I once was given by a client about 10 years ago. She said she thought I would love it and be able to use it in my work. There was no reference of the story at the time, but I subsequently found it by a beautiful monk named Om Swami (you can visit his website for more inspiration: omswami.com). I have added to the original version over the years as I found ways to deepen the process through my decluttering work. It is one of the most powerful release exercises you can do – a practical step-by-step guide to forgiveness, which usually feels like a mental concept.

Be motivated by my clients who have done this process, no matter how hard it was.

CLIENT INSPIRATION

I was fortunate to meet Kate at a ladies' day function and I won the opportunity to be part of her Ignite Your Life course. I was very excited to be able to spend time learning from her, and in doing so I was able to make some significant shifts in my life.

One of the key learnings for me was the importance of letting go of some unpleasant emotional baggage from my past (my "potatoes"). This was a difficult process for me, but at the end of it I felt lighter and able to move forward with courage. I made some significant changes in my life, namely leaving the security of corporate employment to start my own business.

Every time I hear the Katy Perry song *Firework* I am reminded of the life-changing lessons I learned from Kate during this program.

TR

MORE CLIENT INSPIRATION

I did the Ignite Your Life course with Kate in 2012 and it changed my life. I was in a place of confusion, not knowing where I was going, and feeling very unsure of myself. It was tough to commit to the course and to completing all of the tasks, but as it went on, it became easier. I became more and more confident in my abilities and started to re-ignite my inner flame.

Two of the sections stand out for me, even after all this time. The potato exercise was a freeing, inspirational exercise that assisted me to let go and cut the ties with all those people who had crept into my space and were dragging me down. My potatoes traveled down to Durban on a family holiday as that was when the exercise came into play, and the fact that I was lugging my 'tatoes on holiday was the cause of lots of laughter, questions and looks of absolute incredulity. But the feeling I had when I got rid of them was one that words can't describe. I felt relieved, free, strong, confident… everything I had lost touch with and that made me me.

The other amazing exercise was creating a vision board, something that I had heard of, but never done. When the things on my board started coming true in my reality, I realized that if I place my focus on what I desire, I become the creator of my reality. One by one, the rest of the things on my vision board came into my life.

To say that the Ignite Your Life course is something everyone should do doesn't do it justice. It is hands-down the reason I am where I am today, with the confidence I have and the excitement to live my best life ever.

Nicole Philipps

YOUR POTATOES

Was it a pain in the butt to lug your load of potatoes around for a week? Did you feel silly? Did they get too heavy? Did your potatoes even start going a different texture, maybe a little soft and slimy?

Most importantly, what insights did you have about all the people you have been carrying around, the people that in some way have transgressed you? What do the potatoes represent to you?

Now stop and contemplate: would you have been able to carry around all the potatoes without the bag? Yes or no? So what does the bag itself represent to you?

As you know, everything in this course is about ditching your glitch so that you can ignite your life again and get your personal flame glowing strongly within you. When we are still holding onto things from the past, it has a negative effect on us. They are like a heavy weight tied to us, dragging us down at every level. They are your potatoes. And they are held together solely by you and your mind, which is what the bag represents.

FORGIVING A KIDNAPPER

You might have heard about the events that transpired at Groote Schuur Hospital in Cape Town in 1997. Celeste and Morne Nurse had just been gifted the birth of their first daughter, Zephany. Three days after she was born, Celeste recalls half waking from her sleep and seeing a woman dressed in a nurse's uniform standing next to her bed. When she later woke up fully, her baby girl was gone.

The parents never gave up hope of their daughter returning to them. Morne said, "In 2010 I told the media that I can feel it down in my soul that my daughter is out there and one day she will return, so I never gave up." Each year they celebrated her birthday with a cake. Zephany was always brought into conversations and her life was spoken about.

Fast-forward 17 years to 2015. Celeste and Morne's second daughter had just started at a new high school. She saw a girl that looked identical to her and told her dad. After an investigation and DNA testing a few weeks later, it was confirmed that this girl is in fact Zephany. Zephany was placed in social care, as it's a very complicated case.

The couple was interviewed by the radio station Cape Talk, and the most powerful aspect to me is how Zephany's birth parents have already forgiven the woman who kidnapped their daughter.

Celeste said, "If we don't forgive, how are our lives going to move on? We will be stuck in darkness, so in order for God to forgive you, you must forgive too and God will bless you. That is what I have done, I forgave her. Even if I see her I'll give her a hug and say thank you for raising my daughter."

HELL-BENT ON HOLDING ON

What do you need to let go of, and whom do you need to forgive?

The hurts and anger we carry are internal, and all too often we don't consciously see the negative effects or even feel the real weight of holding onto them. We just live with them.

You can bet that you are bearing the negative consequences, but you may be too attached to (or unaware of them) to let it all go. Sometimes we feel so vindicated in our point of view when we have been wronged, and it can actually feel quite nice to be pissed off with someone, blame them for something, keep them at a distance to punish them, feel that intense resentment or desire for revenge towards them. We can feel quite self-righteous and smug about it. "They did this to me!" we think.

It can even give us something to focus our negative attention on, because perhaps we are scared that without all this anger, we won't know who we are or where to direct this energy. Anger and pain can define us. But what is the real cost for us in the end?

Over the years I have gone through this process to heal my spirit and heart. I had failed businesses, broken hearts, fights with my dad, betrayals, letdowns... Just like you! Forgiveness has allowed my life to be more at peace today.

YOU CAN LET IT GO

You could actually be using that very same amount of energy differently and re-directing it towards something positive, such as your dream in life and your goals, which are waiting patiently for you to step up and claim them.

I've had to let go of the regret of not fully appreciating my dad while he was still alive. I always acknowledge what he gave us at a material and home level and how clever he was at business, but I never appreciated enough of who he intrinsically was. I came to realize we were so similar that we were at loggerheads emotionally. Now, I find I can access him at a spiritual level, and I will often have conversations with him, as my grown-up wiser self. I'm no longer the little girl hanging on to my pain. Once I let go of that, I was free to access him in a new way. I hear his voice now, giving me encouragement, advice and support. It is profound for me.

But the longer you hold onto past hurts, the less likely it will be that you reach the level of internal control and success that you say you desire. Perhaps it is finally time to face some of this stuff and shift it? Unleash that energy. That way you can give yourself permission to come back to being fully present in your life, freeing up creativity and space in your heart to move on to the things that really matter.

FORGIVENESS DOESN'T MEAN IT WAS OKAY

One of places where we all get confused is that we mistakenly believe that if we forgive someone, we are actually condoning their actions, saying that what they did or said was okay. And that doesn't feel right because we have been genuinely negatively affected by what has happened.

But it does not mean this at all.

When you forgive someone you are not condoning anything they did at any level. When you forgive someone, you are healing yourself, and it has nothing to do with them. They need to do their own healing and that is not your job. Forgiveness is never about the other person, it is actually about you. But when you are holding on to the pain, you make it about them and what they did to you.

When you are able to somehow, in some way, forgive someone else, you are not condoning what they did. What you are saying is that you are no longer willing to carry around the pain and hurt their actions have caused you.

Read that again, as it is vital.

In this way, you are responsible for holding onto the past, or letting it go. That is your choice. Can you see the difference? It can feel so impossible to forgive someone, yet the energy and lightness that you will feel afterwards is what will allow you to take leaps and bounds in your life. Is that worth doing it for?

The truth is that you can never understand or even get a glimpse of the real reasons someone has said or done something to you, and at the end of the day it does not matter. What does matter is whether you are still carrying that old energy around – your bag of potatoes.

PUT DOWN THE POISON

> *"Resentment is like drinking poison and then hoping it will kill your enemies."*
> Nelson Mandela

Can you even begin to imagine what might not have happened in South Africa if Madiba had not been able to forgive what had happened to him? While we may not yet be free from all the pain of our country's past, and while we face many problems, we have made incredible steps, some forward, then back, more forward then a few back again, just like your own cycle of change.

Do you recall the conversation at the start of the book about how all behavior has a positive intention if you dig deep enough? Our own positive intention when we hold onto fear, hurt, anger, betrayal, resentment, etc. can be to protect ourselves so that it will not happen again, or so that we won't trust that particular person again and thereby get hurt again. It protects our glitch. It can be about survival, keeping our inner-child safe and many other personal reasons.

And yet the nature of holding on to those negative emotions will, in fact, attract more of the same stuff to you. If you are holding tightly on to that place of pain inside, it is so hard to see the joy and gifts that are in front of you. Your beliefs that you will have layered around all the hurts will ensure that you keep getting more of the same experiences, so you will see and feel more pain. There comes a time when it is vital to let all that stuff go, to forgive in a way that releases you from the pain and to finally heal. But for this you have got be willing to let go of what you have been dragging around.

GOODBYE, POTATOES

Because of the difficult nature of this exercise and the fact there is usually a lot of healing to do, I suggest you go gently and take a few days to go through this process. It is powerful and will catapult you forward – yet you have got to go through it. Please do not shy away from this exercise today, thinking you have plenty of time to complete it. How much time do you honestly have? I know that putting it off seems like the easier way, but to light your fire and keep it alight requires boldness, guts and sheer determination to face the yucky stuff. I know you can do this, so please start today, no matter how difficult it may be for you.

"None of us can change our yesterdays, but all of us can change our tomorrows."
Colin Powell

Keep the following in mind as you work through this:
- You can do the process with the person face to face or over the phone using the same steps set out below. Always remember that you need their permission to work through this with them and this is not about dumping all your emotions on to them.
- If they are not willing or able to participate in this process, if they are deceased, or you do not feel ready to engage with them, you can do the exercise on your own, speaking aloud as if the person is sitting across from you, or write them a letter. Complete the process by throwing away, burning or burying the letter to symbolize closure.
- If the other person is able and willing to do this with you for mutual healing, you can both follow the same steps by yourselves, writing it in your journal, and then share it, step by step. It is definitely easier to have it written out and then read it, so you have your own guideline to follow. Do your best to be honest, not to be right.
- If your potatoes are still separate in your bag (as I mentioned they sometimes become slimy) you may want to pull the relevant one out and dispose of it in some appropriate way when you have finished your process. You might want to keep all your potatoes till the very end, and then have a ceremonial bonfire and cook your potatoes to totally transform them. You can also plant them, or smash them with a hammer (this is very effective). Or you can throw them at something (just not the person whose name is on that 'tato) like a target in your garden.
- But you have to do the forgiveness process first.

Here's what we're going to do
Light your candle and set the following intention by writing it out in your journal in your own handwriting, and then sign it. In blood! Just kidding, pen will do.

> Intention: I am willing, no matter how challenging and painful it may be, to feel all the feelings that I have been bottling up, to find peace in my heart and freedom in my soul. I am willing to release all this baggage I have been carrying around, as it no longer serves my highest good.
>
> *So be it.*
> SIGNED: _____

While this process feels very private, ask for help. You could ask someone specific – perhaps you know a very compassionate person – or it may be someone in a religious context, such as God, angels, fairies. It doesn't matter who or what you ask. Just ask for help in a way that resonates with you at every level.

This is the process I follow to bring everything out in the open and then release it. The trick is to keep moving and to keep flowing, not to get stuck in the anger, blame or nasty feelings, which is probably why you have been carrying it around for all this time in the first place. We are working through to the forgiveness and healing on the other side. Ready?

We are going to deal with one potato at a time.

1. Start off by giving the pain and hurt around this person or incident a number from one to 10. One means you feel at peace and totally calm; 10 means you are like a raging fire of anger, hurt and vitriolic feelings, and you possibly even want to hurt the person.
2. Write about any denial that you may have felt. I know in the past when something has happened to me, I have first gone, "I can't believe this is happening, it can't be true!" I can get stuck there. Write it down.
3. Next acknowledge how you really feel or felt at the time. Really vent as much as you possibly can about why you are angry, hurt, disillusioned, bitter and full of resentment. Start sentences with "I'm so angry that...", "I'm so mad...", "I'm pissed off because you..." I find that swearing can sometimes help at this point. Just spit it all out – better out than in!
4. Write the following phrases in your journal and complete the sentences in the way that feels right for you. Take your time and remember to take some deep breaths.
   - I'm so irritated that...
   - I'm hurt and saddened the most by...
   - I expected that... and so I feel...
   - This has made me question several things...
   - If I put myself in your shoes to understand what happened from your perspective, I imagine...

- I'm sorry for… and I didn't mean to contribute to this by…
- I am now grateful that…
- I now know for sure that…
- I forgive you and I release you for…

When you've finished, wash your face and re-assess how you feel from one to 10. If you feel you need to do the process again, you can, but perhaps another day.

When you have processed your potato, keep repeating to yourself, "I am free!" Decide what to with the physical potatoes to signify the end of this process.

Please note
Take your time to really feel all your emotions with each person. For real healing and forgiveness, you need to put yourself back in the situation, feeling your pain and acknowledging where they were coming from, too.

If, for any reason, you feel you cannot face some of this right now, perhaps starting to write a letter will take you to the next level. Sometimes it can help to have a friend come and sit with you, just to be around for support. You do not need to speak to each other, they can simply be in the room with you while you go through this process.

You may find flower essences such as the Bach Flower Remedies useful at this time as they help you shift your emotions in a gentle way on a vibrational level. A great one to start with is Rescue Remedy, which assists with stress and shock.

Get professional help if you need to. In some situations, and depending on the nature of the hurt you feel was inflicted on you, you may need to get additional professional support to complete this process. See the stepping out section for some ideas for resources to try. Don't be scared to ask for professional help as it can help so you move through this with ease. There is strength in knowing when something is too big for you to face alone.

This might also be the time to find me and a community of supportive fellow beings on the online community. The details are on page 22.

> *"People are often unreasonable, illogical, and self-centered; love them anyway.*
> *If you do good, people may accuse you of ulterior motives; do good anyway.*
> *If you are successful, you will win false friends and true enemies; succeed anyway.*
> *The good you do today will be forgotten tomorrow; do good anyway.*
> *Honesty and frankness make you vulnerable; be honest and frank anyway.*
> *What you spend years building may be destroyed overnight; build anyway.*
> *People really need help but may attack you if you help them: help people anyway.*
> *Give the world the best you have, and it may never be enough; give the world the best you've got anyway."*
> Mother Theresa

This newly released energy can now fuel your life, your fire and your goals. Breathe in that awesome possibility right now.

Time to reflect

"When you are clear, what you want will show up in your life, and only to the extent that you are clear."
Janet Bray Attwood

I trust you are feeling lighter and brighter after getting rid of your potatoes at last? Clients constantly tell me that they start evaluating life pro-actively after this massive cleansing process, and they instinctively know when they are starting to collect a new potato. They also report being able to not let them accumulate, or to have the courageous conversation about what is happening that much sooner. Just knowing that something could become a potato if left unheeded galvanizes them into action. I guess the sheer dread of having to go through this full exercise ever again is enough to keep you on your toes.

ACTION PLAN 3

How has the rest of your week been, taking action in line with your goals? You'll see there is a slightly altered action plan to use for your week ahead. Remember that you can use your own system, so long as whatever you are using is helping you to keep it all at the forefront of your mind and assisting you to take action in line with your goals. There is no right or wrong way, just the way that works best for you. Whatever system you use, ensure that every day you are looking at it, ticking off items of action, reading your goals and new beliefs to support your goals, spending a little time journaling, rating your fire energy and living with healthier boundaries.

This week, there is a space on your action plan to add your top three values.

YOUR AMAZING ACHIEVEMENTS

Let's take a little time to recap and summarize all that you have been through so far. When you look back and see everything that you have done, you will be amazed!

Use the summary below to pat yourself on the back and remember all you have done, as well as to find any little gaps that you may have been slipping up on or forgetting about altogether. Put them back on your personal radar. Remember how you rated your personal fire at the start, and how you have been re-igniting it.

1. You kicked off by taking stock of your entire life as it was at the beginning of the book with the cycle of life exercise. Usually this reveals all sorts of wobbles and unhealthy situations in your life, depending on your circumstances. It's great for finally being honest about where you are, rather than hiding your head in the sand. You were also introduced to the art of gratitude journaling every day, as well as a simple way to rate your life out of 10 and then do something practical to shift it immediately. You have been challenged to do these actions daily for the duration of the book, and they are great little actions to keep up, even on the days when you feel you can't get around to the rest of the exercises. A little step forward is just that: a step forward.

2. Then you asked people you respect and trust for some feedback and insight to help you understand yourself better.
3. The next step you undertook was to write a letter to yourself about your cycle of life from your wiser self, to gain another perspective into yourself.
4. You went another layer deeper to find the glitch that you have been operating from in life. Knowing your Achilles' heel is the first step to letting go of it so that you can concentrate on shining your light and being more you.
5. Your inner-child came out to play with your vision board exercise. And ideally that is up somewhere visible, along with your goals, and might even be on your smart device as your screen saver. That, for me, was one of the game changers, as I was able to look at it every time I looked at my phone. My phone was recently stolen, and, when it was replaced after 10 days and everything was reloaded, I literally kissed my vision board screen saver. It made my heart sing!
6. Next you chose the three areas of life you wanted to actively work on and shift, and learned how to write goals in an effective way. You were also given several questions to unpack your goal a bit more, and got to grips with the difference between actions and goals. You also had to define how you were going to reach your top three goals, and learned how important it is to place your goals somewhere visible to remind yourself. Your goals whisper to you when you can see them.
7. Next you were given an action plan to help you list your weekly actions in line with your goals, plus a place to record daily that you have been journaling and rating your life. Sticking this somewhere visible boosts your personal accountability tenfold. You were also asked to start finding all your limiting beliefs, especially in the three areas you are working on this month, as these are what trip you up.
8. Then I shared how to create new affirming beliefs to help you powerfully ditch the old ones. These new, positive statements give you the potential to shift and show you a way to move forward, rather than letting the old beliefs keep you stuck.
9. The potatoes! Say no more…
10. The next step was looking at ballsy boundaries and creating a pause between the stimulus and your usual response. We acknowledged that things are the way they are in your life because for the most part you have let them happen, and you are in control of your attitude and how you respond. You were challenged to set healthy boundaries for yourself.
11. Then we elicited your top 10 values. It is important to consciously acknowledge them so you can keep yourself on your authentic track and live according to them. This ensures your goals are really what matter to you. It creates inner peace and happiness. We also spoke about how often people will betray their values to save themselves from facing an emotional fear.
12. We've just completed the second, practical part of the potatoes exercise to forgive those who hurt you, release you from the past and unleash your life, heart and soul again.

How does reflecting on everything you have been working on feel for you right now? Are you chuffed with your progress? Perhaps you can also go back and double check that your actions for the week ahead will really get you to your goals. Give yourself a reason to achieve what you started and have been working on for the past three weeks. It will help you to push through to the end to get what you want.

STEP 17:
Clear your clutter

"Perfection is not when there is no more to add, but no more to take away."
Antoine de Saint-Exupéry

Today I am going to ask you to spend your personal hour doing some physical clearing. To follow on from all the emotional decluttering and heart healing you have just completed, you will intentionally do some clearing out in your physical space.

If you need specific support and guidance with clearing clutter, then you might want to check out my website www.kate-emmerson.com. You will see a link on the home page where you can just click through, and once you sign up I will give you a free week of the Spring Clean Your Life course.

In the meantime, here is some information from my first book, *Clear Your Clutter*.

When you think about clutter in your life, you will probably immediately think about the following kinds of things:
- Stuff that is lying around.
- Your messy desk.
- Rubbish that needs clearing.
- Clothes that don't fit.
- Clothes you don't wear.
- Stuff that is broken.
- Unwanted gifts stashed in a cupboard.
- Anything you are hanging on to "just in case".
- Magazines or newspapers lying around.
- That overflowing drawer, cupboard, room or outbuilding.
- Too many things in too small a space.
- Lack of organization.
- Etc. etc…

DEFINITION OF CLUTTER
Whether we are referring to outdated clothes, messy paperwork or limiting beliefs, all clutter has the same underlying energy. Simply put, clutter is anything that no longer serves you, for whatever reason.

THE THREE CATEGORIES OF CLUTTER
Physical clutter
This clutter is everything that is tangible and visible; the messy stuff that takes up all the physical space around you. This clutter clogs up your actual living and work spaces.

Physiological clutter
Your body has several internal cleansing systems, such as your blood, lymph nodes, kidneys, liver, skin, bowels, etc., and if they are not working properly they will literally clog up the space in your body, and steal your vitality.

Energetic clutter
This takes up emotional, mental and spiritual space in your life, and thus drains or zaps your energy, thoughts and time. This clutter blocks up your emotional space. Your potatoes fall into this category.

HOW DO THESE FORMS OF CLUTTER AFFECT YOU?
Time
You waste time looking for misplaced things, shuffling through piles of paper, always running late, hurting deeply about emotional issues so you are never present, worrying about unfinished business, being absent from work – or, when you are at work, being unproductive, doing everything slowly with no enthusiasm – lying in bed longer than necessary every morning as you feel weighed down, mucking about with email due to your poor organizational systems.

Money
There is a very direct cost in having too much stuff. You have to allocate funds to keep it clean (either doing it yourself or paying someone to do it for you), insurance for all those goods, store it all (either in your home or in extreme cases having off-site storage facilities) and the high cost of transporting it all if you move.

Clutter bugs commonly buy food, toiletries and clothing in triplicate (purchasing yet another black top, more sneakers, an extra jar of chutney to join the four half-filled bottles in the cupboard and a tenth deodorant) simply because they don't know what they have or where it is buried. What a waste of money!

Also think about the cost of poor financial habits, the interest accrued by paying bills, fines and taxes late.

Sometimes you will find money hidden in your neglected belongings. How much more cash is stuffed in old pockets, ornaments or books?

Energy
Living with any form of clutter wastes your energy, leaving you feeling dull, lethargic, clogged up (often in the literal sense of the word) and with zero vital energy in your body. Hiding behind your clutter means you are hiding from life, playing small, burying emotional pain and getting stuck in your past. Your attachment to anything that no longer serves you steals your energy.

You also won't live mindfully in the present. I have never come across clients who have clutter who do not also suffer from massive stress in their lives. It is common for clutterers to be on antidepressants.

Creativity

When you live with clutter you cannot think clearly, will have no inspiration and will feel so overwhelmed that it becomes impossible to formulate new ideas or creative solutions to problems. You cannot see exciting opportunities as all your "stuff" blinds you.

The trend is procrastination, and the pressure of everything being behind schedule zaps creativity. Living with the fear of not being able to let go at the right time, you tell the universe you do not trust that all will be well.

Reputation

Clutter creates feelings of shame, deep embarrassment and zero sense of control, and you constantly berate yourself for this. This results in you being late for meetings, renegotiating deadlines for projects, forgetting facts, never feeling in charge, always being flustered and highly stressed. You feel totally disorganized and unprofessional.

The sad truth is that people judge us, whether they are right or wrong, on what they first see and experience when they meet us. If your clutter is affecting your professional life, then your reputation, career and relationships could be at stake. Imagine a prospective boss, exciting potential client, or gorgeous new date being able to peek into all aspects of your life, both those seen and unseen. Would they be dying to meet or hire you, or dying to run a mile?

HOW TO DO TODAY'S EXERCISE

See if you can relate a physical space to the internal themes you were forgiving people for. If you were to give a theme to the forgiveness exercise, or perhaps to your biggest potato, where would a corresponding physical space or object be in your home?

- If your theme of potatoes and forgiveness centered on your poor self-esteem due to what has been done to you, it may be a good idea to clear out something like your clothes closet, letting go of old items that do not serve you anymore. Poor self-esteem can cause you to dress inappropriately for your size, age or career. Ensure that you let go of anything that does not support the new direction your life is taking. Donate or sell things that no longer need to be in your space.
- If your forgiveness work was around relationships, betrayal, infidelity, divorce, etc. it might be time to let go of old diaries, letters, journals, photos or sentimental mementos, but only if you feel ready. Doing this will signal the release from this old energy. An interim step could be to pack stuff up and put it in your shed or garage. In six months, you might be ready to let it go. Make this work for you.
- If you worked with a lot of stuff from when you were very young, look around your home and see what you might be holding onto that is part of that old

energy. It could be a soft toy, an ornament or something really small that holds that energy. Or perhaps you could display a photo of you when you were unbelievably innocent and joyful, rather than having one from a time that was painful. You could also consider doing a full clear out of photographs, letting go of all old ones that attach you to a painful time in your life.
- If your forgiveness was about money – perhaps someone stole from you, or you from them, maybe they cheated you or a business failed – what could you clear out that would release that old energy attachment? Consider clearing out the physical place where you keep all your bank records, your admin and your purse. Check that your will is up to date and all the beneficiaries of any policies are correct. Or perhaps you need to help someone else get started in a business as a way to clear this energy. Trust yourself to know what to do.
- If your forgiveness was around your weight or being teased about your body, then perhaps you could look at clearing out your clothes, shoes, make-up and toiletries, or do something else related to the image that you present to the world. Consider what's in your kitchen cupboards and the literal aspect of food and nourishment. Or start a detox program.

Trust yourself to know what physical space in your life corresponds to the healing work you have just completed and let yourself tackle that area today. That way you are making another powerful intentional statement to the universe that you are ready to move on.

It is also very useful to play beautiful and inspiring music while doing this exercise, having your candle lit and maybe even some incense or aromatic oils burning. It will create a very gentle sacred space in which to do this.

Have a beautiful clutter-clearing day.

My story

When I was about 28, I lived in Barrydale, a lovely little village, in the Cape. I had followed my spirit to the village when I was introduced to it by two friends who had moved there, and ended up living there for a year. I was managing a retreat center while it was being completed, and it was one of the most introspective, contemplative years of my life. I did have a few wild parties at the infamous hotel and with locals, but mostly it was a quiet time. I left that village just three times in the entire year.

While I have mostly been a minimalist all my life (my love of traveling always inspires me to keep possessions to a minimum), I have written journals since I was 13 years old, pretty much every day of my life (I told you journaling was important!). I still had my black trunk from boarding school with all of that stuff in it. I had been doing some profound clearing, cleansing, healing and forgiveness work, just like you are now, and I "woke up" one day and realized that I didn't need to hold on to all those photos and diaries from the past. I poured a large glass of wine, lit a big fire in the garden braai (barbeque) and decided it was time to start letting go of some of the stuff from my past that was encapsulated in this trunk. I had recently said the first goodbye at a conscious level to a very good friend, as we were seriously no longer good for each other. It had been such a relief to post that letter to say goodbye, and now there was more to do. I set about doing a mammoth burning session. It might not have been that great for the environment, but I needed it to burn, baby, burn!

I re-read some stuff I'd written and looked at photographs and let go of 80% of the contents of that trunk. I decided to keep a few pictures – just ones that made me happy and fulfilled. I burned the diaries I'd written from age 13 to 21 with love and joy in my heart. My main spiritual awakening started at 22 when I traveled to Southeast Asia, so I kept diaries from those years on for insight and clarity. It was such a release and I have never regretted it. I did it with intention and it was liberating beyond belief.

MY EMOTIONAL CLUTTER

If you have ever heard me giving one of my talks, you may already know the story of how I fell in love with my best friend. It's never really a pretty situation if they don't feel the same way about you. I bet you are either giggling or grimacing if you have been in this situation. It went on for about 18 months, until I realized that he was becoming clutter in my life.

I slipped a disc in my spine in 2013, and the chiropractor told me in no uncertain terms that I had two letters to write – one to my dad and one to "the man in my space". Because honesty and courage are my two highest values (and I knew the pain of not being honest about my bulimia all that time ago) I had already realized that if I were to die, I would have regretted not having told my friend how I felt. So I had already come clean with him; we had spoken about it a couple of times and it was starting to completely de-rail and debilitate me. I was yearning for him to realize he felt the same way, or hoping that he'd touch my arm when we had coffee; I was even dreaming about him. He would suddenly overtake all my thoughts, such is the power I was giving him. And all the while I was putting my heart on hold.

As I was lying flat in pain, crying from the agony and totally drugged up, I knew I had to let him go. I also knew that there were three possible outcomes, and all of them were better than the trajectory that I was on:
- He might realize he felt the same way.
- I'd get over it and if he could too, we'd be able to be friends again.
- I'd find space in my heart to love someone else.

It was time to let go. I couldn't even sit up to write the letter, I had to lie on my back and type. He knew it was coming. I am eternally grateful that two and a half months later I was able to phone him up one day to just say, "I miss you". We are still friends to this day. If I hadn't let him go to free myself from the shackles of my emotions, I cannot fathom where I would be today.

Letting go is not easy, but it is necessary. I know people look at the stuff I teach and the insights I share about clutter and assume I have every aspect sorted. No, I'm human. You also have stuff that is easy and stuff that is hard. I have just found it easier in that I believe the work, I trust the process and I have witnessed the healing work in my own life and my clients' lives.

So, who or what do you need to clear out today to spur you along this path? It's time to get rid of it. My wish for you is to be brave and do the decluttering you need to do to bring your energy and spirit in alignment with your life. If you need some more inspiration, contact me on the private Facebook group. The details are on page 22.

STEP 18:

Boost your bucket before you kick the bucket!

> *"Dream as if you will live forever; live as if you will die today."*
> James Dean

Let's face it – nobody is guaranteed to make it to tomorrow. An idea I love from the deck of cards titled Buddha, by Osho, is that if you are trying to live your life too safely, you never truly live, and conversely, if you attempt to live without any risk, you metaphorically die long before your death.

Today we've got a fun exercise. You have been actively working towards three goals for the last few weeks, and it can be quite normal to start thinking about what lies next for you, beyond this initial shift. And if you haven't been doing that, then today is the day to pay attention to it. Life is really beginning now that you have ignited your fire, and keeping it alight and creating a blazing bonfire is an ongoing quest.

The moment you start paying attention to your life, you will begin thinking, "What is next for me? Are there some other things I wish to explore? Is there more for me? Do I want to aim bigger than what I am striving for now?"

Because you are becoming more and more in charge of your life, you might be realizing that you have been playing small for too long, letting life dictate to you rather than you dictating to life. So today we are going to change direction a bit and start thinking about your dreams and your bigger picture again.

> *"It takes no more energy to have a big dream
> than it does to have a small dream."*
> Jack Canfield

Go to a brand new page in your journal and title it: My Bold Bucket List. Colored pens and crayons work fantastically for this kind of creative list – so let your inner child come and play once again.

This is a similar exercise to your vision board (but remember in that exercise I asked you to think about the year ahead and what you wish to manifest), but your bucket list has no time frames. Perhaps next year a lot of these bucket list items will get onto your vision board so you can activate them by making them concrete goals. Every year I come back to read my bucket list, to add new experiences to it and to decide which ones to activate for the coming year.

My story

One of my bucket list items is to see the Grand Canyon and Sedona in the USA, and quite by chance I got to visit them when I went to Las Vegas for my film. It just happened out of the blue, as I wasn't actively working on that this year. Your vision board and bucket list will shape your life as you let them come alive.

NO LIMITS

Your job today is simple: to hold the idea that time and money are totally irrelevant, and to listen to your heart and soul's desire. As you hold those two things as true, write down 100 – yes, a hundred – things that you really, really wish for. Be big and bold! Slay those voices of the limiting beliefs that may be surfacing as you read this. Look at what you have already achieved in the past few weeks alone. You are in charge of what you get out of life, so keep asking, "What do I really, really want?"

Come and post the top five things on your bucket list on the Facebook page to inspire yourself and us. You never know who can help you reach your dreams when you share them. Ever since my dad told me what an amazing country Argentina is, going to Buenos Aires has been one of my bucket list items. It's on my vision board to go dancing there, and just recently I met someone from Argentina, and I'm thinking how wonderful it would be to visit with a native of that country… I'll keep you posted!

Think about all eight areas of life, every facet of your being and the things that really excite you. Think about the kind of work you might like to do, the places you want to see, the people you would love to meet, the personal goals you want to achieve, the difference you wish to make, how many kids or grandchildren you desire, where your ideal home is. Maybe there are languages you would like to learn or instruments to play. What about swimming in every ocean in the world, learning to meditate in a Himalayan monastery, going scuba diving? Or seeing whales swimming, hot air ballooning, riding across the USA on a Harley Davidson (another one of mine!)… Do you want to read all the books by the classical authors, or attend live shows by your favorite rock stars or classical musicians, write a book, speak to audiences about global warming, grow your own veggies, break a record, become the president? What do you wish to have on your list?

There are so many incredible things to do, see, feel, touch and experience, and the starting point is simply having the guts to say that you want them.

CHALLENGE 1

The trick with this exercise is to have no limitations whatsoever. Imagine that you can have your life any way you want it – what do you want it to include? Let your desires run wild.

I suggest that you sit with wonderful inspirational music playing, light beautiful candles and incense, eat some delicious soul food, and then give yourself an hour to dream your dreams and write your list of 100 items, or more if you are on a roll.

TIP: If you find that you battle to write your wish list, play the "game" from the movie, *The Bucket List* and imagine that you have just one year to live, yet you have all the money in the world. What would you put on your list then? At first it might seem that all the things are materialistic, so be honest and think about the things that give you deep fulfillment. What about the satisfaction of finally doing a huge presentation at a world conference, marrying your soulmate on the beach in the Maldives, seeing the glimmer in someone else's eye when they too realize a dream, the warm feeling of helping an older person through a difficult time, or giving an abandoned puppy a home? This is about what makes your heart and soul happy.

CHALLENGE 2

Watch *The Bucket List* with Morgan Freeman and Jack Nicholson as soon as possible. If you have already seen it, perhaps you can invite some friends over and watch it again to get some more life inspiration.

CHALLENGE 3

Chat to at least two friends over the next two days and ask them what their dreams and wishes are to see the kinds of things that people long to be, do and have. If your friend has not done this exercise, perhaps you can make an evening out of it and do it together. Remember you start with one, get to 10, then 100!

RISK

Love & risk being hurt
Give & risk being taken for granted
Help & risk involvement
Speak out & risk disagreement
Be different & risk criticism
Make a valid attempt & risk failure
Climb & risk falling
Truly live & risk dying
LIFE IS A RISK
Those who avoid all risks are avoiding life itself
Indeed life's greatest risk is not to risk at all
Sally Eichhorst
Dare to Succeed by Warren Veenman and Sally Eichhorst (Reach Publishers, 2013)

SHARE IT

I'd love to know what's on your bucket list, so please tell me on our Facebook group. The details are on page 22.

STEP 19:
Face your false fears

> *"Courage isn't having the strength to go on, it's going on when you don't have the strength."*
> Napoleon Bonaparte

You are getting close to the end of this process. Is that exciting or scary?

Today I would like to look at the topic of fear, which is usually a direct manifestation of your glitch. This is the last little sticky bit we need to address to assist you to ditch that old junk once and for all and keep your fire burning brightly. Fear is like a large hosepipe spraying water over your personal fire, but only if you let the tap get turned on. If there is any fear in your life, along with self-limiting beliefs and negotiated boundaries, and if you are not living in alignment with your values, you will continually be tripped up and glitched up.

Fear and self-limiting beliefs are linked and often feed each other, but they are different. We have fears about things that we want to avoid, and fears that we simply create and enlarge in our minds. A self-limiting belief gets created around the fear to protect us from even trying.

For example, we can feel that we are scared of rejection or fear intimacy and vulnerability, and the typical beliefs that can arise from that are:
- I am no good at relationships.
- I will never be understood by people.
- I'm too old to get involved again.
- I don't have time for a relationship.

Then that belief gets embedded and starts driving all our thoughts, words, feelings and actions in an endless loop.

TAMING THE MONSTERS

When you start taking control of your life, there comes a time when you will have to face your fears. You cannot grow yourself, your family, your business or your dreams without confronting your false fears. We all have them, and most people will do anything to avoid the feeling of fear. Are you one of those people? If you are, you can say that you want things in your life till you are blue in the face, but you will have to face your fears at some point along the way to achieve your goals.

I think that facing our fears is actually a natural part of our progression, and it forces us to continually expand and confront things in our life. Overcoming them makes us stronger, more resilient, and gives us a huge kick of self-achievement. It is where there is so much room for growth and potential. So please do not shy away from the things that you fear. They are really never as bad as you make then out to be in your mind.

It is all an illusion really. FEAR as an acronym stands for False Evidence Appearing Real. In other words, most of what we fear is not really true at all. We make our fears out to be worse and bigger than they actually are, and then they become monsters in our lives. But monsters can be tamed, changed and ultimately killed.

FEAR IS NATURAL BUT NOT ALWAYS NECESSARY

Please don't for one second assume that successful people do not have fears; that is a false assumption. Everyone has fears, but the real differentiator is whether you let your fears dictate to you, or whether you act in spite of them. That is the simple difference. Susan Jeffers wrote a book called *Feel the Fear and Do It Anyway*. That's essentially what we have to do.

So yes, there is a difference between healthy fear that is trying to protect us and alert us to danger, versus our self-inflicted fears that keep us playing small. In the olden days, well really I mean the cave days, we were conditioned to respond to harmful outside experiences with either fight or flight. That absolute need for survival is very different for most of us nowadays, yet we still live with the remnants of that primordial fear in our bodies, even when situations are not really life threatening. When we have that fear response, adrenalin surges through our body, and if that happens for too long (which is common nowadays as we live in self-inflicted fear of many things) then there is a constantly heightened level of adrenalin in our body and it means that we lose the ability to differentiate between real danger and self-inflicted fearful thoughts. That adrenalin triggers the release of cortisol, which simply keeps us in constant stress mode. We need to then find stress-releasing exercises to shift the cortisol and adrenalin.

My story

About three years ago, I decided to do something wacky, crazy and adrenalin-filled, just for the sheer hell of it. There is something called "rap jumping", which is an insane high-energy sport in which you jump face first off the top of a building. I had heard about this at a networking meeting and decided to look up the guys who did this wild stuff in Johannesburg. I was told I could jump the following Sunday and I found myself driving into town, fairly wide eyed but determined to do it anyway.

The building, in a dodgy part of downtown Johannesburg, was derelict and had very few occupants. It wasn't the most reassuring start, but nevertheless I was resolute, as were the other souls that collected there.

Just getting to the top of the building was pretty hair-raising! We had to climb through a window, cross over an open drop on all fours, shimmy up a rickety ladder and then take a decrepit lift that creaked and groaned to the 25th floor. Then we walked up another set of iron stairs and along a narrow passage at the side of the building where someone was waiting for us.

We were wrestled into girdle-like harnesses, and given very strict instructions on safety and how to use the ropes. First you have to walk up three steps, (well, waddle in the harness), sit your butt on the ledge of the building with your legs dangling over the edge and walk down the building until gravity takes over. Oh, and have fun while doing it!

Just swinging my legs over the side put my heart in my throat, before I even looked at the ground. The only thing between you and ground is one thick rope, which is monitored by someone at the top and bottom. Basically, you get hoisted over the edge and then – picture this – you are looking straight at the ground below you! My feet were against the side of the building and I was looking down, with my body parallel to the ground and perpendicular to the building. Think Spiderman but way less sexy! I started feeding the rope and walking, and then I felt gravity kick in. You can let the rope go faster, and even push a bit away from the wall.

Oh, oh, oh! My breath was short and my heart was pounding in my ears – yet the adrenalin felt so good! The second time I jumped I shimmied a bit faster. But just before the third time, something interesting happened in front of me.

There was a young couple who had just gotten engaged. The man had done lots of rap jumping before and wanted his fiancée to experience it. She was a proficient abseiler – where you face the wall or rock face – so I assumed she had no fear of heights. He decided that she was going to go first, so she was hoisted up and as she sat on the edge of the building just before she was about to be whisked up and over to face the ground, she burst into tears and started shaking and trembling.

The fiancé looked embarrassed and just a little concerned. He asked her what the hell was wrong and told her she should just do it. It was his need that she jump, not hers. He started to get irritated and it was so interesting for me to see someone who was essentially not afraid of heights, yet she just could not face it in this slightly different sport. He wanted to pressurize her to jump before the guy in charge told him to back off and leave her alone.

I always wonder if they ever got married or if that was something that could have pushed them apart. I assumed that she would just fly off over the edge with wild abandon, yet her fear took over. Or perhaps it was mimicking something emotional that was transpiring within their relationship, and which got played out on the building ledge that day. Make no mistake, there is a real fear of death when you do these kinds of sports. It's part of the high that you get.

FIND THE TREASURE

We never know where our fear comes from. Sometimes we are asked to face our fears to go through to the other side and find the reward, and sometimes it really doesn't matter whether we do or don't do it.

To get more insight into fear, imagine a lovely carved wooden door with a shiny brass knob. Standing in front of this doorway are two huge monsters with long, sharp nails, scary fangs, fire coming out of their mouths and beady, glistening eyes. Their lips are curled back and they are snarling, ready to attack you.

Why are the monsters at the door? What is their purpose?

When I ask audiences I'm addressing this question, people say, "They are there to scare us", "We've put them there", "They are our imagination"…

All of that is true, but the real, underlying reason why there are monsters or guards standing at an entrance is that there is treasure on the other side of that door.

Imagine that this metaphorical door represents a fear of public speaking and nothing in your body wants to get up and give the presentation to 20 board members tomorrow. You and I can walk towards the very same door; although I have some apprehension about public speaking, I will be able to flick the monsters on the nose, open the door and walk through it to give my presentation. You, however, with a massive fear of public speaking, will only see the monsters snarling at you. What kicks in in that exact moment is primal fear. I have always considered FEAR to be an acronym of F#@$ Everything And Run!

Typically you will turn tail and bolt, and not face the fear. You are outta there!

All of the things that we are afraid of, we make ourselves be afraid of, and by overcoming them we give ourselves the opportunity to be free. We tend to make the fear bigger than it really is and by simply taking one little step at a time, we can slowly overcome the fear.

My story

I used to detest any form of being on stage and hated drama at school. After playing Christopher Robin at age eight and singing solos, I lost my nerve and never volunteered for productions. The only time I did was for a big one that gave me lots of time off school. I was just one in a crowd and wasn't noticed.

I never fancied doing those talks in front of the class on a subject or any kind of public speaking. I never aspired to be a prefect, and one of the many reasons I left boarding school at the age of 12 was because I was told I would be head girl if I stayed there. I didn't relish that at all, either the leadership or having my life carved out for me. Talk about stubborn!

Fast forward to the time when I was a professional life coach setting up a new business and the idea of leveraging my time and energy started intriguing me. While I appeared confident and had a can-do-anything attitude – I could easily talk to people at a networking group, strangers at a cocktail party, and a small group of people – the idea of standing up and giving an inspirational talk to an audience of 50 people or more was a scary thing for me. But I also knew with all my heart that I wanted to do bigger talks. I felt compelled to.

So I scaled down the risk. I started doing small workshops for about five to seven people. Then I progressed to small talks. Every year I took on bigger and bigger audiences and I have now gotten to the point where addressing 1 000 people is fun for me. But it required one incremental step at a time. Now I am conquering the fear that surrounds talking to a group of 5 000. Yikes, that feels big!

Starting small and taking little steps closer to your goal actually makes facing your fear fun.

WHO'S GOING TO WIN?

We all have fears, and we can all overcome them. What one person can do, another can too. You have to ask yourself, "Am I willing to fail trying, or am I going to try failing?"

The thing is, if you are not prepared to fail by at least trying, you will never reach your juicy goals and you will be destined to play small. Do you really want that? If you let fear run and ruin your life, then you will be 100% assured of failing and your inner fire will slowly die completely (and it gets harder to re-light every time).

Let's say you are scared of failing at something, so your intention is to protect yourself, and then you do not even try because of your fear. But that automatically means that you have failed because you will never try, so failing becomes a given. So you have fulfilled your own fear by simply giving in to it and not trying to achieve your goals. Does that make sense? So who is in charge here – you or your fear? Don't let your fear be bigger than you!

NAME THEM

You need to look at all the things you are fearful of and bring them out into the open. What exactly are you afraid, fearful or scared of right now? Maybe writing your wonderful bucket list of 100 dreams has brought some stuff to the surface. Or maybe you couldn't even put some things down because of the fear? Perhaps…

- You want to visit the Grand Canyon but you don't live in the US and are scared of flying.
- You want to speak at an international conference yet are scared of being laughed at.
- You really want to scuba dive at the Great Barrier Reef but fear being under water and relying on a tank for air.
- You want kids but are scared of committing to marriage or single parenthood.
- You want to enter the Cape Town Cycle Tour yet are scared of not finishing or falling off your bike at the start.
- You want to start a business but have no degree.
- You want to move to a new city but don't know how to start over again.
- You want to be in a relationship but are scared of getting hurt.

Well, the truth is that your fears will stop you in your tracks if you do not face them. Often, overcoming them can be as simple as naming them and setting yourself little challenges or goals that will ensure you overcome them. That way, to achieve the goal, you have to face the fear. For example, if you set the goal of visiting the Grand Canyon and even book your flight, then you will have to do the work to get over your fear because you have committed to the goal. You could start by taking a short domestic flight or two, before embarking on your big trip.

FACE THAT FALSE FEAR

So let's do something practical to help you face the fears. Remember, our fears are mostly self-generated, which means we can also find evidence to counter balance them. Are you willing to put it all on the line for your dreams?

You may need to give up your fears to get the life that you want. This is how.

Write them down

Make a list of all the things you are scared to do. It doesn't matter what they are, just list them, no matter how silly you may feel writing them down. No one is looking, so be honest.

Ask your partner or friends if they know anything you are scared of or intimidated by. If you look back at the original feedback you gleaned from those eight to 10 people, you might get some clues.

Work through them

Use the following nine-step process to help you examine your fears. Work with your fears one at a time. I suggest you do two or three today and some more tomorrow.

1. Write down what you are scared to do, for example, "I'm scared to ask X out on a date."
2. Rate your fear on a scale of one to 10, with 10 being the worst it could possibly be.
3. Consider why this scares you and makes you afraid. Is it rejection? Being alone? Being laughed at?
4. State it as a sentence with the following phrases: I really want to... (fill in your fear) and then I want to run away because I...
5. Now ask yourself what is the very, very worst thing that could happen if your fears were actually to come true. If you wanted to ask someone on a date, you might write:
    - They could reject me.
    - They could laugh in my face.
    - They could spread rumors about how desperate I am.
    - They could already be married.
    - They could totally ignore me.
    - And then I wouldn't have a date for the wedding and may have to go alone.
6. Next ask yourself what emotions that worst-case scenario would bring up for you. Possibly loneliness, unworthiness, rejection, abandonment or feeling less than.
7. Then ask yourself what inner and outer resources you possess to help you handle all of those terrible things anyway, even if all of them happened. This really helps you to turn the fear around and put you in charge.
8. Now gather information on how you can lessen the potential pitfalls so that you do what you fear anyway. Maybe you'll write:
    - I know X has gone out on other dates.
    - Other people have said yes to me.
    - I could ask a friend if X is open to dating.
    - I don't have a date with X now, so even if they say no, I haven't lost anything.
    - I could ask them what their favorite hobby is and invite them to something that will excite them.
    - Nothing ventured, nothing gained, so I will go for it anyway!
9. Take one action towards overcoming your fear, so decide what that first step is and just do it.

"Fear is that little darkroom where negatives are developed."
Michael Pritchard

All of this helps you to get more rational about your fear so that you can do something in spite of it.

Let's look at another example, using the same exercise as above. This time you have a money-related fear about property investment:
1. I am afraid to make the wrong property investments.
2. Eight.
3. I could lose my money, have bad tenants, become over extended with high interest rates, the property could be in the wrong area.
4. I really want to invest in property and then I run away because I am scared that it is all going to go horribly wrong and I will lose all my money.
5. I could lose R100 000 and have to start all over again, I could have cash-flow problems, and I would have to sell my property to recover my costs.
6. Failure, inadequacy, "lack of" mentality, frustration.
7. I know that I am actually good at doing my homework analytically, I am resilient and I have reliable gut feelings.
8. I need to go on property investment courses, read 10 books on property investment, speak to people who are doing it well, start small and build my experience as I go rather than starting too big and making costly mistakes, only invest money that I do not need for immediate cash flow, ask an accountant to help me understand the figures and only buy cash positive properties. I must do my homework thoroughly.
9. The first thing I will do is book a place on a property investment course on Monday. (Then add it to your action list.)

You need to be willing to stand up for the life that you want and to confront the dragons of fear so that you can start turning your dreams into reality, achieving your goals, and then reaching for even bigger and more meaningful ones. Overcoming your fears is a necessary step along this path, and it is so worth it.

Now go and play with your fears. They are just little monsters that want some attention from you, so give them some attention, and then put them to bed so you can get on with your life and start thinking about how to step boldly out into the world.

Remember that I want nothing more than to see you succeed. If you want some advice or guidance, ask me on our Facebook group. The details are on page 22.

STEP 20:
Pull out all the stops

"You either move toward something you love or away from something you fear. The first expands. The second constricts."
Tom Crum

It is time for you to complete your final action plan 4 (page 156) as you charge towards the finish line and get that fire roaring inside you. How does this feel after all your effort and work over the past few weeks?

Today, you need to look at what absolutely must be completed this coming week for you to reach the three goals you started off with.

There will be no excuses, no "what ifs", no bemoaning that life got in the way, or saying that so-and-so poured water on your fire… This is the week to pull out all the stops, no matter how busy or tired you are, or whatever else is getting in your way. You started this course with powerful goals; if you have gotten this far then you have already put so much effort in. Now it's finally time to give yourself the opportunity to achieve them. Do you have you any idea how amazing it will feel when you reach that place?

Do you remember the 90/10 rule from Step 9, where we made our action plans? Here's a reminder:

The first 10% of time that you spend planning and organizing your work, before you begin, will save you as much as 90% of the time in getting the job done once you have started. What a bonus way to find more time in each day by simply pre-planning.
Brian Tracy

That very same energy and intention applies as you focus all your attention on the last leg of this phase of your personal journey. The hour that you spend today on looking back at what action you have already taken and what still needs to be done will stand you in good stead for the rest of the week.

TODAY'S EXERCISE
Evaluate
Go back and look at your action plans from each week with all the accompanying things that were added, such as your new beliefs and values. Take a look at how well you have done and where you have possibly slipped up. If there are any outstanding actions that you have been carried over, can you catch up and complete everything this week?

Follow the plan
Do you remember all the wonderful questions you answered about your top three goals in Step 8? You looked at all sorts of things including your "why", benefits, consequences, resources etc. Go and pull all of those answers out and re-read them now.

What was the plan that you came up with in terms of how you are going to achieve these goals, what your strengths are, and who you could be accountable to? When re-looking all your responses, is there anything that can give you some tips for completing this last little bit of your journey? Perhaps you have forgotten something, let something slide, or simply overlooked something that jumps out at you now as you re-familiarize yourself with what you wrote just a few weeks ago. Remember that a plan is only as good as the extent to which you follow it.

So what do you need to pay special attention to this week so that you will fly over your finish line with a big grin on your face that signals your huge achievement? This is the week of closure, so make it work for you as much as you can.

Look at action plan 4 and notice that there are a few different aspects to it this week.

Goals
Boldly write your goals in the blocks.

Original %
Fill in the original percentage from your very first cycle of life for this area.

Today's %
Rate today's percentage as it is right now.

I am just ….% short of my goal of ….%
Fill in the shortfall between where you are right now and what your original goal for the end of the five weeks is. For example, I am just 5% short of my goal of 60%.

This gives you a very clear picture of what has to be achieved in the next few days. How are you going to achieve this last bit, no matter what? Use everything in your power to achieve it and make sure you add it to your action plan.

Add to your action plan
Notice that there are a few new headings in the last columns. Look at each one and see if it can help you to add some new actions to ensure you reach your targets. Do you want to be basking in the light of your own fire and swinging from the treetops because you have done what you set out to do? It takes vigilance, application and dedication.

As you find the answers to these questions, remember to add them to this final action plan so that you can tick them off as you accomplish them.

Who can help me?
Is there someone you can call on this week who will assist and support you as you reach this goal? How can you enlist their help? Can I help you with anything to get to your destination?

The boldest thing I will do to achieve this goal
C'mon, c'mon, you have been working on your self-limiting beliefs and fears, so what is the one thing you know you need to do this week? The thing you need to do to just go for it? You know in your gut what it is, so I am challenging you to do it!

"I have been impressed with the urgency of doing. Knowing is not enough; we must apply. Being willing is not enough; we must do."
Leonardo da Vinci

Courageous conversations and ballsy boundaries

Remember I said that being too negotiable with your personal boundaries and simultaneously reaching your goals is not possible? They are normally mutually exclusive.

If you are battling to reach your percentage targets, what are those difficult conversations you still need to have with yourself and others to get back on track immediately? Which personal boundaries do you need to re-enforce? Just because you have told someone something once does not mean it necessarily sticks. You have to be true to your convictions and stick to them to ensure others take you seriously. Are you taking yourself, your goals and your values seriously enough?

Big reward

This is the week to celebrate all your hard work. This is what makes it more fun. If you have not been doing your rewards so well each week, this is the one week that they are non-negotiable. Make sure you give yourself a huge pat on the back and reward yourself in some amazing way for all that you have accomplished.

SOME INSPIRATION

You have to believe that you can do this. I dare you to believe that. In fact, I double dare you!

Remind yourself of your positive beliefs, your values in life and why all of this is really worth it for you. Do not give up, do not let others get in your way and do not procrastinate on your goals. Get your plan together and get cracking.

The Facebook group is there to support you as you do this work, so please share your journey with me and the community. The details are on page 22.

You can do it! You really can! Here is some inspiration:

Our deepest fear is not that we are inadequate.
Our deepest fear is that we are powerful beyond measure.
It is our light, not our darkness, that most frightens us.
We ask ourselves "Who am I to be brilliant, gorgeous, talented, fabulous?"
Actually, who are you not to be? You are a child of God.
Your playing small doesn't serve the world. There's nothing enlightened about shrinking so that other people won't feel insecure around you.
We are all meant to shine as children do.
We were born to manifest the glory of God that is within us.
It's not just in some of us; it's in everyone.
And as we let our light shine we unconsciously give other people permission to do the same.
As we are liberated from our own fear, our presence automatically liberates others.
Marianne Williamson, A Return to Love

Part three
Stepping out

"If one advances confidently in the direction of his dreams, and endeavors to live the life which he has imagined, he will meet with a success unexpected in common hours."
Henry David Thoreau

STEP 21:
Shine your light

It is time to step out into the world and claim your place in it.

Now that you have put all the effort and time into yourself and put yourself back on your priority list, what happens next? This is a critical time, and it can sometimes feel so much easier to slowly shrink back into your original comfort zone – unless you choose not to. You have been pushing and expanding your boundaries of possibility, and now it's time to go up another notch.

YOUR THERMOSTAT

Think about the thermostat setting on the air-conditioning or heating unit in your home or office. It is set to a specific temperature. No matter how hot it is outside that room, or how many bodies are jam-packed into it, the thermostat is designed to homeostatically, through systems feedback, keep that space at the temperature that is set on the dial.

Only if you change the setting on the dial will the temperature change. You know that! You don't sit there wishing the room was a different temperature. No, you press the remote and change it. Your life is the same. Your original thermostat was revealed when you completed your first cycle of life. You have now upped the ante through doing all this work and have pushed the temperature of your thermostat up with every step. You have locked this in as your new default setting, and it will only go back to the old setting if you choose to let it. Your frame of reference has changed, so let's keep it that way.

TODAY IS THE DAY

I personally find that this process of getting used to your new thermostat setting and choosing to keep it set high is the most delicate one to navigate. You need to be bold as you step out.

If you have not yet joined the Facebook group, which is available only for people who are doing transformational work with me, then do so now. You'll find all the details on page 22.

Public platforms of the right caliber are profound in helping you stay accountable. I know there can be lots of negativity and invasion of privacy with social media, yet if you use it correctly and discerningly, it is a sacred space of sharing. People on my Facebook group are making shifts in their life, so come and join us, blow your trumpet of change, and ask for support when you need it. I challenge you to come and share what you have achieved. Step out into the world and claim your space.

GOD IS LIKE THE WIND

We cannot see the wind, but we can see the activity it creates;
Moving through the trees, rustling the leaves, blowing over grasses.
Likewise with God, for though God is invisible and unseen we can perceive the effect of God's creative force in our lives.
In the miracle of birth, in a mother's unconditional love, in the joyous laughter of a child.
Even when there seems to be no wind, if we are very still we can feel the wind's presence.
Similarly with God, for in those moments when we doubt God's existence, if we are very quiet and calm we will feel God's omnipresence.

When the wind blows very hard, if we are moving very fast, we may not be aware of its strength.
Likewise with God, if we are very restless and busy we may not sense God's presence even though it is omnipotent.

If we disregard the re-balancing force of a strong wind, it may blow more powerfully in the form of a hurricane or tornado to fulfill its purpose.
Likewise with God, if we ignore God's omniscience in re-balancing our lives, God's will may be more forceful to bring us back to purpose

It is always our option to heed the forces of nature and hear the message in a gentle wind, or we can wait for a gale wind to get our attention.
Similarly with God, we can listen to God's whisper, or we can wait for God's shout.
It is always our choice.
Don Glassey

MAKE IT JUICIER

You might realistically and quite rightly be on a huge high after achieving all your goals, so take time to celebrate and enjoy your rewards, but don't be foolish and pretend that things will stay rosy forever.

This is life, and life is tough. Things will get in the way, issues will crop up and people will test every part of your newfound inner strength.

Accept that. Don't simply pretend it's all pussycats and gentle rain. There will be wild tigers and hailstorms. This is when your character will define the next step. Are you going to go into cruise mode, or do you want to live an even juicier, more fulfilled life of grace and ease?

You have so many tools at your disposal now – use them.

CLIENT INSPIRATION

I found Kate because I was beginning to drop some critical balls. I had started my own business, was newly married, was building a house and had two Jack Russells.

It was much more than I could juggle.

My new wife was not enamored with me working all day and night. The business was moving ahead but it took all my time, weekends too. The dogs were ignoring me and the house I was building was not going according to plan, which started hurting my back pocket.

When I met Kate we spent a few hours together so she could understand me and my situation. I decided to expose everything to her as she gave me the feeling that it was okay to be totally transparent. By the end of those first few hours, Kate had shown me a way to manage my stress, visualize my perfect day and, even more importantly, find a path that could help me bring balance into everything I had on my plate.

I knew it was going to take some work. There were days that the exercises and homework seemed like mountains. Not because there was too much to get through, but because the tasks and challenges Kate set before me were personal mountains, things I had steered clear of in the past. I could no longer run away as I knew Kate was going to question me about these things and she knows how to dig deep.

I was not alone in the process. There were other people on the course with me and we all committed to meet on Skype at 5 a.m. We reported back, and encouraged one another and fought through the pain. And there was pain! There were times when some of us were in tears and some of us got angry but we all helped one another through, and with Kate's support and compassion, we all walked our paths to the end.

My time management did a 180-degree turnaround. My business flourished, I completed building my house, my wife was only too happy to hear me drive into the garage at 6 p.m., and even the dogs were there waiting for their daily run with me!

I have a new philosophy because of Kate's process, that balance creates balance and once you are in balance, you can get through anything and everything.

To this day I use the tools I learned on the course in all aspects of my life. Sure, I forget them sometimes, and when I realize that I have a tool to change something, I kick myself for not using it sooner. Am I perfect after making use of these tools? No! But I am a lot less imperfect. I still push myself too much and sometimes I realize I have let an area of my life slip, but I correct it. At times I realize my confidence has waned but I know how to fix that too. And at times I have started on the same path of making an old mistake, but I pick it up a lot quicker now and change that path.

I will continue working with Kate, not only because she has an amazing transforming effect on my life, but because I want to be a better person and she has a magical way of showing me things I sometimes never even knew existed.

Brett Preston

SHINE YOUR LIGHT

To step out with panache, it will serve you well to be vigilant with your life and your dreams.

- Be beautifully and authentically you.
- Have big goals, yet surrender to the outcomes.
- Deal with stuff as it comes up – swiftly. When you fall down, just notice it faster so you can get up quicker.
- Get rid of all clutter in your life.
- Speak your truth with kindness.
- Do your best. Take 100% responsibility.
- Live as if today is your last day. Live lighter and live larger.
- Step out with effortless grace and ease.
- Know when to push, know when to release. Know when it's not your battle. Do this no matter what anyone else thinks.

- Trust your instinct and act on it.
- Shine your light as you are the only one who can.

When you feel your power shrinking, or you start giving your power away, come back to the basics. Light your candle, get your pen and paper and start journaling.

I always start off again with gratitude journaling, followed by the cycle of life.

My story

About three years ago, my best friend shared with me what he thought my glitch was: a combination of Push Pushier Pushiest and Worthless Worth. The two were playing together in perfect ironic harmony. Over a glass of wine, he said he witnesses me coming out all guns blazing, stepping up, forging ahead with new ideas and yelling BOO! And then I run away from my dreams, goals and ideas – super fast. I let fear get the better of me and I believe those monsters at the door that I spoke about.

At first I was taken aback – harrumph – but then realized that this friend was, in fact, 200% right. My desire to expand, just like yours, always demanded that I stepped up, yet after I had voiced it, or started putting things into action, I would shrink again and find a reason not to do it.

It was the way he described me running around saying BOO! that made me see the funny side.

There is such power in hearing someone who loves you unconditionally give that form of feedback from their heart. For me, it became a concept I could actively work with so that I could change it. I know it wasn't easy to ask for feedback from those eight to 10 trusted people right at the start of this journey, and perhaps if that is one exercise you skipped, this could inspire you to do it now. Insight given with wisdom, compassion and love is profound.

I am now much more dedicated to saying BOO! and then keeping on in the direction of my dreams. I do less running away, or perhaps more realistically, I run for much shorter distances while I let the fear settle. Once it's quietened down, I come back. It's a process.

Remember I shared my story about stepping out in a bigger way at the beginning of 2015, with the new CRM platform and database management? That was me saying BOO, BOO, BOO! I was playing bigger, being bolder, and following my dreams of reaching more people. I had put the name of the platform, Infusionsoft, on my vision board, knowing I would shift over to it during the year. What happened after that was astounding. Two weeks after I started shifting across, from that Monday evening when I committed to them via Skype, I got invited to join their annual conference in Phoenix, which happened to be one week before I was going to be filming in Las Vegas. I just smiled and laughed, realizing how I had brought this up on my radar through the RAS (reticular activating system).

Was I scared? Hell yeah, because it put me on a whole new level. Was I ready to step out? Double hell yeah, because I can't run anymore. Boo! I went to Phoenix, attended the conference and saw the Grand Canyon and Sedona.

Sometimes we have to trust our life and the bigger picture, and get out of our own way!

YOU HAVE THE TOOLS

Do you ever say BOO! to the universe and then, instead of surprising it, you end up running away with your tail between your legs? What would happen if you didn't run for as long and as fast? You might scare the living daylights out of yourself, but hey, you might also realize your wildest dreams too.

I believe that part of what holds us back is the fear of not being able to do all the bits required of us to get to where we want to go. We make it seem bigger than it really is, coupled with that shouting voice in our heads that tells us we will fail, we aren't good enough, blah, blah. You have tools to face this head on now. You can sort out limiting beliefs, pack a bag of potatoes, and do the fear exercise. Use your tools.

LAST PRACTICAL EXERCISE – YOUR CYCLE OF LIFE

Look at your original cycle of life and the goals you achieved while working on this book. Now it's time to think bigger.

Re-draw your cycle of life for today on a blank page in your journal, or use this one, and then answer the questions on page 128.

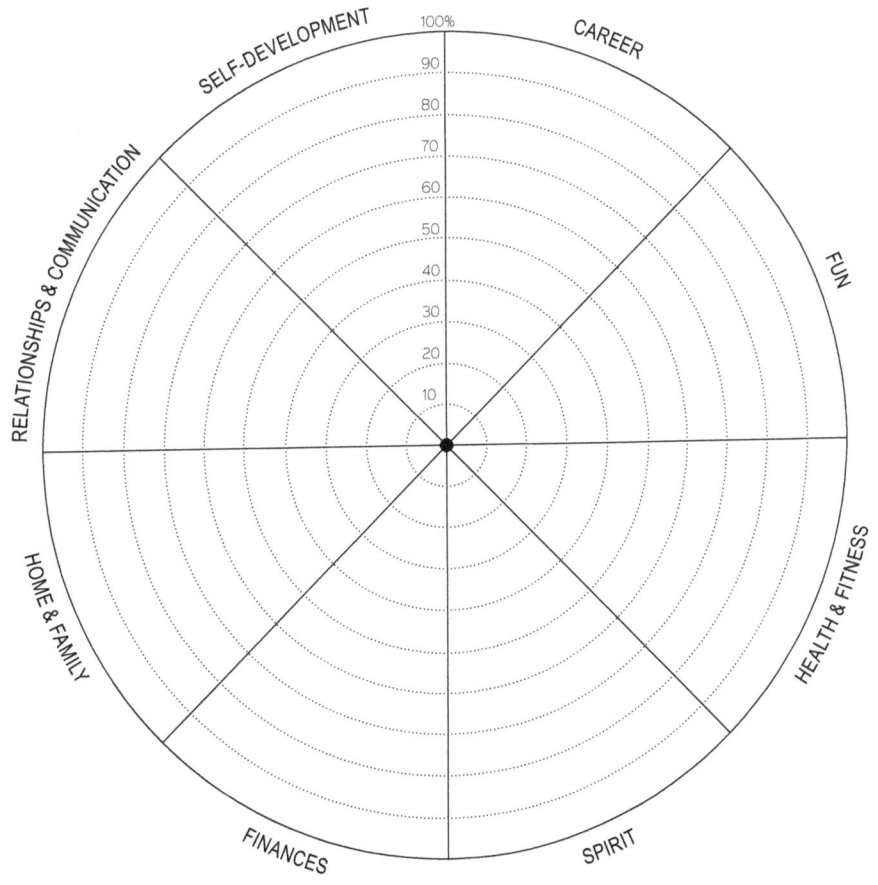

Stepping out

1. What is the one word that describes your whole life today?
2. How does that feel compared to when you started this journey a few weeks ago?
3. Have you managed to reach your target percentage in your three areas of life?
4. How do you feel about the shifts and progress you have made?
5. Although you have been actively working on three areas of the cycle, have other areas of life have also improved because you have reclaimed control?
6. How does experiencing this knock-on effect feel?
7. What's next? I suggest that you give yourself some new percentage targets to reach two months down the line, in all eight areas of life.
8. Look at your vision board right now. What can you commit to that will help you manifest something on it?

STEP OUT BOLDLY

- Share your big goals on the community platform.
- Share your goals with at least one person who will help you stay accountable.
- Hire a life coach, join a mastermind group or get a mentor to keep you on track.
- Contact me on www.kate-emmerson.com

Healing modalities

People often ask me how I manage to keep on track, stay upbeat, handle the stuff that comes my way, bounce back, accept, grow...

Over the past 25 years, I have used a variety of healing modalities, which I want to offer to you as resources. I never offer up processes or ideas to clients if I have not tried and proved them for myself. There are a gazillion more available, but these have crossed my path, and maybe they will support you on the next step of your journey.

But let me clarify something. I am not implying that you need to seek out external things because there is something inherently wrong with you. I do, however, feel that there are times when we all need some help and support along the journey, and we may do well to look at different things at various times in our lives.

Come to terms with the fact that you are perfectly imperfect, a wondrous creature that can self-heal, expand and grow. Your spirit is immense and beautiful. It is only your human "crap" that holds you back, but it also holds the key to transformation. A lot of the work we do is about letting go, surrendering, remembering and undoing the layers so we simply get back to the real you.

So if you need help, get enough to get you back in alignment, and then move on. Do your best not to get stuck on any one healing modality, otherwise it becomes a negative dependency, even when it's natural. Know when it's time to wean off – whether it's from medication or your alternative healer. Trust your body and your spirit and know when to help it along its path. Be a great custodian of your spirit in this body of yours.

These are some of the tools that I have personally called on in my beautiful journey to happiness and wholeness, the road I walked to get back to the real me.

HOMEOPATHY

This system of medical practice treats a disease with minute doses of a remedy that would in larger amounts produce symptoms similar to those of the disease. It's based on the principle that like treats like.

Homeopathy works best for treating the unique symptoms of an individual, not for a diagnosis given to many, which is why a number of people use it as an alternative to conventional treatments. Homeopaths can treat conditions that do not necessarily fall into a particular "disease category".

AROMATHERAPY

My first love of alternative healing – fragrant and delicious plant extracts. Aromatherapy uses plant materials and aromatic plant oils, including essential oils and other aromatic compounds, to alter a person's mood or cognitive, psychological or physical wellbeing. It's based on bringing the body back into balance. While writing this book I have been using rosemary oil to stay alert, awake, focused and mindful. When I go to sleep, I use lavender oil to chill and release the day's energy.

Although the word "aroma" makes it sound as if the oils are inhaled, they are usually massaged into the skin, either by being mixed with creams and oils, or added to baths, compresses and inhalations. You should never take essential oils by mouth without specific instruction from a trained and qualified specialist.

OSTEOPATHY

For the past year this has been my preferred treatment for holistic transformation, and its effects have been profound for my growth. It treats more than the body, truly incorporating the psyche, spirit, heart and mind. It's a drug-free, non-invasive manual treatment that focuses on total body health by treating and strengthening the musculoskeletal framework, which includes the joints, muscles and spine. Its aim is to positively affect and balance the body's nervous, circulatory and lymphatic systems.

This therapy is a unique holistic approach to health care. Osteopaths do not simply concentrate on treating the problem area, but use manual techniques to provide overall good health and wellbeing, including the "breath of life".

CHIROPRACTIC

Having been exposed to chiropractors when I shared rooms with well-known practitioners in Durban, I have to say that my first experience of this modality was not a good one. I was then exposed to network chiropractic, in which the treatment is gentle, intuitive and energetic, rather than manipulative and "spine cracking". However, two years ago when I slipped a disc and couldn't walk for a month, I was guided to a fabulous chiropractic healer. I was told I could either go straight to hospital to have an MRI scan and a spinal operation, or I could get some drugs for the pain and inflammation and trust the chiropractic treatment and healing process. I went every week for five months as having an operation was not an option for me. There is a time and a place for everything.

Chiropractors diagnose and treat misalignments of joints, especially the spine. When the spine is out of alignment, it can cause problems in the rest of your body, as the spine is your nerve center. By correctly aligning the vertebrae, you can improve wellness, sleep better, boost immunity, reduce stress and improve cognition.

REFLEXOLOGY

This is another love of mine and I have studied and practiced it. Reflexologists apply pressure to certain points on the hands, feet and ears that correspond to specific parts of the body. It is particularly good for treating areas of the body that are not easy to touch, such as the internal organs. Reflexology benefits both body and mind.

REIKI

This profound, yet gentle, way to treat the whole body originated in Japan. Traditionally it's used to reduce stress, but it can also boost overall healing for body, mind, emotions and spirit.

It is a form of energy healing in which the practitioner will lay their hands on the patient to transfer life force to them.

CRANIOSACRAL THERAPY

This feels like your whole brain is being cradled and loved. Craniosacral therapy focuses on balancing the flow of fluid in the spine and brain. Through therapeutic touch, the joints in the skull are manipulated. The effect is overall wellness, improved vitality and a happier, healthier you.

EFT

I'm a practitioner of Emotional Freedom Technique (EFT) and it's one of my all-time favorite modalities as it is a simple tool you can learn to shift emotional blocks. Sometimes people call EFT "psychological acupressure" because you tap on certain parts of your body as you focus on a particular emotional problem. The points where you tap are the end points of energy meridians, which allows the emotional energy to be released.

NEUROLINGUISTIC PROGRAMMING

I studied Neurolinguistic Programming (NLP) to complement my life coaching skills, and so I understand the profound effects it has on changing our internal frame of reference and shifting us into excellence. It is about creating empowering new thoughts to help us improve our lives and interpersonal relationships.

In some ways it is similar to self-hypnosis as it also has certain principles about how language and eye movement affect the brain. Great for re-patterning beliefs.

BODYTALK

This non-invasive natural healthcare system uses the wisdom that your body holds. Practitioners use physical feedback to see where imbalances and blockages lie, which can then be treated, allowing your body to regain health and wellness. It taps into your body's natural ability to heal itself. Helps to tap into unconscious patterns.

BODY STRESS RELEASE

This technique is more hands-on than BodyTalk, but it's similar as practitioners also use gentle physical tests to find the areas in the body that have stress locked into them so that it can be released. It's a truly advanced approach to natural healing. In my experience, it's a gentle form of specific muscle and tissue manipulation, yet it's deeper than massage.

KINESIOLOGY

This is great for uncovering specific blockages, past traumas, allergies to certain foods and so much more. Your hand is used to get muscle feedback in the form of a positive or negative response from the body to find, heal and shift the imbalance.

Kinesiologists treat a range of conditions including stress, muscular disorders, nervous disorders, allergies, nutritional deficiencies, emotional problems and learning and behavioral difficulties.

MASSAGE

Oh, if I could go for a massage every week I would. Never underestimate the power of a great massage. There are several different techniques, but basically the soft tissue of the body is manipulated, which improves circulation, reduces stress and boosts vitality.

Ask around to find great therapists, trust your gut and let your body go to heaven as it relaxes. Try Swedish, Thai, sports, kahuna, etc.

ACUPUNCTURE

This has really helped me manage pain in my back and sciatica. With a crack in my spine, known as spondylolisthesis (which was why I closed my aromatherapy and massage practice), and my slipped disc, acupuncture has been invaluable in my tool box. Fine needles are inserted into the skin at specific energetic points on the body to treat a whole range of physical and mental conditions.

TRADITIONAL CHINESE MEDICINE (TCM)

This is an ancient holistic system of health and healing, based on the notion of harmony and balance. I was introduced to this when I got sick while traveling in Asia. The focus is on healing and prevention of disease by using diet, acupuncture, herbal medicine, massage, and exercise. Try it!

IRIDOLOGY

This was initially a bit of a weird one for me, but just as reflexology treats people through reflexes in the feet that correspond to the whole body, iridology is the analysis of the iris, which is the colorful area of the eye that surrounds the pupil, as areas of it correspond to the rest of the body. By analyzing the iris, a person's health problems can be diagnosed and appropriate remedies can be given. The amount of information that your iris can reveal is fascinating.

BACH FLOWER REMEDIES

This is my first port of call when I'm dealing with emotional transitions, stress and hiccups in life. These beautiful flower remedies were developed by Dr Edward Bach in the UK. He believed that the underlying emotional condition of patients was a major contributor to their state of disease. After researching the healing properties of wildflowers and herbs, Bach identified 12 "healers" and 26 "helpers" for a total of 38 remedies in all, which relate to a particular characteristic or emotional state.

They work very gently at a vibrational level, and the most popular one is Rescue Remedy, a combination of five remedies to treat shock, pain and trauma. I carry this with me all the time, as you never know when someone will need it.

ENNEAGRAM

I am new to exploring this personality system that emphasizes psychological motivations. The Enneagram is a model of human personality, which is made up of nine interconnected personality types. It's a wonderful tool for diagnosing your psychological outlook on life as it provides a fascinating tool for self-understanding.

MEDITATION

If there is one practice that is becoming widely used and spoken about, it is meditation. It is about concentrated focus on a sound, object, visualization, the breath, movement, or attention itself to increase awareness of the present moment, reduce stress, promote relaxation, and enhance personal and spiritual growth.

Meditation benefits people with or without acute medical illness or stress. People who meditate regularly have been shown to feel less anxiety and depression.

Just get started. Find a class, or join an online group such as Deepak Chopra and Oprah who regularly offer online courses. Don't overthink it, get practicing!

YOGA

This is an Eastern discipline that includes breathing techniques, meditation and physical poses. Yoga is my exercise of choice and I urge you to try the many different forms of it. There's Bikram, Flow, Iyengar, Forest, Hatha…

Be open to trying it and you will experience increased body awareness, stress reduction, mental calmness, better breathing, less pain, better joint health and balance, improved strength and a whole lot more! Yoga keeps me sane on all levels – body, mind and spirit.

TAI CHI

This is great for über-stressed types who need to chill out and re-connect with themselves. It's an ancient Chinese tradition that, today, is practiced as a graceful form of exercise. A series of movements is performed in a slow, focused manner and accompanied by deep breathing. Don't let the speed fool you, though. Tai Chi is a martial art that is known for its defense techniques and health benefits.

It's an effective way to alleviate stress and anxiety as it's really meditation in motion.

VISION QUEST

The ceremony of the vision quest is a powerful Native American rite of passage to find spiritual guidance and purpose. To access this deep understanding of your life purpose, you usually go away into the seclusion of a wilderness to receive messages from nature and your spirit.

FAMILY CONSTELLATIONS

I used this particular modality to help understand some family lineage issues I was grappling with, particularly as a woman in my family. It was profound for me because it helps to break destructive family patterns of unhappiness, illness, failure and addiction. The results are often immediate and life changing. It is a group process that has the power to shift generations of suffering and unhappiness.

Family Constellations help heal illness, resolve conflicts and solve problems by releasing blocks in our unconscious mind that prevent or limit our health, growth or happiness.

THERAPY AND COUNSELING

To have a neutral, candid, supportive professional give you a different perspective and tools to help you cope is invaluable in life. Please seek professional support if you need it to resolve any personal or psychological problems.

In therapy, you meet with your psychologist or counselor to discuss and resolve problematic behaviors, beliefs, feelings or relationships. It can address a wide range of mental health issues such as depression, anxiety and grief, particularly at times of transition.

DEMARTINI METHOD

Dr John Demartini has created a scientific process that balances perceptions and emotions. One of his well-known techniques, which I used with a therapist when I needed some support, is the Collapse Method. It's a great tool for gaining instant insight and creating transformation so that you have an empowered and inspiring life. It helps to reduce stress, resolve conflict and create new perspectives and paradigms for life.

THE SEDONA METHOD

This is another simple, powerful, easy-to-learn technique that allows you to uncover your natural ability to let go of painful or unwanted feelings. The Sedona Method consists of a series of questions you ask yourself that lead your awareness to what you are feeling and gently guide you into the experience of letting go.

AURA-SOMA

This amazing modality involves numerous bottles that are mesmerizingly beautiful and mind-blowingly powerful. It uses the energies of color, herbs, crystals and gems. You choose any four colored bottles from a wide variety, and they take you on a journey of self-discovery. Try this once in your life!

INNER CHILD WORK

This is about talking to your inner child, which is the aspect of you that loves fun exercises, like the vision board, playing silly games, and eating pizza and ice cream. I remember when I first started a conversation with my inner child – ooh, was she mad at me.

In psychology, our inner child is our childlike self, and it includes all that we learned and experienced before puberty. The idea is that your inner child reminds you of your decisions and behavior as a child and so continually influences your attitude and personality. Healing the inner child is one of the essential stages in recovering from addiction, abuse or trauma.

DO WHAT WORKS FOR YOU

You need to find the tools, ideas, tricks and techniques along your journey that work for you. The above are just a few that have helped me personally, and I use them when I need to.

Please share your experiences with these healing modalities with the online community. The details are on page 22.

Stay vigilant and expansive as you keep your life ignited.

Stay connected: support for your journey

One day, when the time is appropriate for you, you may want to come and work with me and my team in a different format. You can find all the relevant information on my website: www.kate-emmerson.com.

Contact me on shift@kate-emmerson.com for more details and to get started with the next steps on your journey.

FACEBOOK COMMUNITY

If you still have not joined, do so now to be supported as you step out into your life. And if you are already a member, keep checking in to inspire others and be inspired by them.

Join us – all the details are on page 22.

MASTERMIND GROUPS

Of all the work I do – and I love everything – I will always keep doing mastermind groups. The energy of collaboration that happens in a mastermind group is nothing short of profound, for every participant at every level.

If you seriously want to step out and let yourself be counted in the world, this is the most fascinating space in which to do that. Mastermind is a carefully selected group of people who are committed to looking up in their lives. The process facilitates exponential growth in business and personal development for everyone involved.

We challenge each other by raising the bar as we create and implement goals. We brainstorm solutions and interact with each other with total honesty, respect and compassion.

Each participant is a catalyst for your growth. While being your greatest champion, they may also play devil's advocate to encourage you as you catapult your life forward. Imagine the effect of sharing time and space with people who are masters in equal but different ways to you.

RETREATS

I love going with inspirational people (like YOU) to idyllic locations to do transformational work.

Give yourself the gift of time away to regain a sense of balance and self, and come with me and a small intimate group to a breathtaking place.

You find all the details about retreats on the Events page of my website: www.kate-emmerson.com.

BOOKS

My first book, *Clear Your Clutter,* is available on my website www.kate-emmerson.com and Takealot.com in South Africa, and internationally on Amazon.com. An e-book version is also available.

ISBN: 978-1-920479-68-8

ONLINE COURSES

This is a great way to do transformational work wherever you are. You can do online courses in the comfort of your own home, connected to people all over the world. Find out more on my Shop page: www.kate-emmerson.com/shop.

I regularly create free video series to help you tackle a specific challenge, so sign up to my website and I'll let you know whenever there is a new one.

THE SECRETS OF THE KEYS

This is the movie I have been telling you about in this book and I am so excited to share it with you!

What if your doctor told you you're going to die? That's exactly what happens to motivational speaker and author Elizabeth, the main character in *The Secrets of the Keys*. Throughout her career, she's been guiding others, and she has to tap into that same inspiration to make sense of her situation.

Then she finds her own spiritual guide, Gwen, who has an intriguing opportunity for her. Gwen takes Elizabeth on a mystical journey where they meet a range of impressive experts who are eager for her to accept Gwen's unique offer of a new kind of existence.

It's an empowering and transformational film that is both entertaining and beautiful. It will forever change the way you look at life.

It's written and produced by Robin Jay, who has a unique hybrid style of creating a fictional story, to which she adds insights from some of the most respected experts in the field of personal development, including me!

This is what Robin said: "Kate's insights for decluttering our lives so that we can move forward and experience greater joy every day is a message that everyone needs to hear. She's an absolute genius! I know her message will have viewers rushing to declutter their homes, as well as rid themselves of their useless emotions and all the other 'baggage' that has been weighing them down."

I just love hearing things like that!

The Secrets of the Keys stars these outstanding experts:
- Brian Tracy, international business and success guru.
- Rev Michael B. Beckwith, spiritual leader and founder of AGAPE International Spiritual Center.
- John Assaraf, spiritual entrepreneur, philanthropist and teacher.
- Dannion Brinkley, author of *Saved by the Light* and founder of *The Twilight Brigade.*
- Don Miguel Ruiz, author of *The Four Agreements.*
- Gloria Loring, singer, songwriter and actress.

This remarkable film also features these experts from around the world:
- Dr Alfredo Besosa, founder and director of the Mind/Body/Spirit International Institute in Bogota, Columbia.
- Carol Scibelli, speaker, writer and author of *Poor Widow Me*.
- Dr Terry Gordon, cardiologist (retired), American Heart Association National Physician of the Year and author of *No Storm Lasts Forever*.
- William Liu, life coach and transformational leader.
- Leslie Stein, one of the first women to attend West Point Military Academy in the USA, author of *Penny Perspectives*.
- Farida Akadiri, life coach and self-proclaimed "Queen of Manifestation"
- Yours truly, Kate Emmerson.

To order your copies of this inspirational film, go to the Shop page of my website: www.kate-emmerson.com/shop

More client inspiration to support your journey of transformation

FINDING MY INNER KNOWLEDGE
Coaching with Kate has provided me with invaluable tools which I use every day. They may on the surface seem to be common sense, but when one is faced with what seems like an over-whelming task or goal, common sense is never easy to conjure up. I found it absolutely essential to have the support of a whizz of a coach like Kate.

I read the other day that one of the traits that millionaires have in common is that they use the services of those who can help them achieve a better outcome – and Kate to me is one of those people. She assisted me to put things into achievable bite-sized tasks, showed me how to prioritize what's important and held me accountable. She assisted me to find my inner knowledge, talents and strengths and to step through the fear of self-doubt to create a more balanced life of work and play. I now understand that only I can change and through my changes the circumstances and people around me change.

Through her techniques she assisted our company to increase its product line (one of our goals) and produce a better income. I now feel more in control of my destiny and have better focus and energy. Thank you Kate for the fabulous lessons!
Florence Niemann

THE POWER OF MASTERMIND GROUPS
I absolutely love mastermind groups. They are addictive, which is why I have participated in three already. I love getting together with a variety of people from different industries and walks of life who have a common vision of pushing themselves and their businesses to do more and be better. Kate is always inspirational as a facilitator of the group because she does so much herself and always supports and pushes you to do more, to get out of your comfort zone, face your fears and be accountable.

It is an awesome process that is worth every cent. It definitely benefited me as a person and in my business. As a coach myself, it is good to take time out to focus on your own business, stretch yourself and ensure that you are building your vision and your goals while helping everybody else achieve theirs. Thanks Kate!
Dina

GRABBING HAPPINESS WITH BOTH HANDS
Kate: guru, mentor, kick-ass chick!

I was invited to participate in the Ignite Your Life course in Mauritius. To be honest, I agreed only because going to Mauritius has been on my bucket list for as long as I can remember. Having already met Kate when she helped me clear my house, mind and body of clutter, I was familiar with her crazy way of attacking life – head on with an absolutely devilish sense of humor, loads of empathy and the severity of a Mother Superior!

Meeting the other course participants, who were total strangers, at OR Tambo airport was mind blowing. We just clicked, even though we were a right motley crew. Arriving in Mauritius was awesome. It was like landing in heaven.

Our work started in earnest the following morning. We were soul searching, finding out where we stood in life, what we were doing to sabotage our happiness, and how we were enabling others around us to pull us around by the nose. It was a true journey of self-discovery, breaking the shackles that were holding us back from realizing our fullest potential, and grabbing happiness with both hands.

There were days of hilarious fun and days of tears and aching bodies. All the while we were growing, learning to be kind to ourselves and realizing our own self-worth. I'm an enabler by nature, always putting the happiness and needs of others before my own. Changing that has been a battle but, I'm happy to say, I've finally 'got it'.

I owe Kate a huge debt of gratitude for opening my eyes and mind. I highly recommend that everyone attend her courses – I will be on the next one. I have nothing to lose and everything to gain.
Granny Bev

ACHIEVING MY DREAM

After turning 40, I wanted and needed more in my life, but I battled for months to realize what these things were and how to make the changes to achieve them.

This is when I called on my good friend Kate Emmerson to provide me with the tools to assist me make the shifts for me to realize my goals. I attended one-on-one coaching sessions with Kate in line with the Ignite Your Life course. Through these sessions I was able to establish goals in all aspects of my life. I also learned so much about myself and the reasons why I was stopping myself from achieving these goals.

I first had to figure out what was standing in my way. I realized that I was definitely not a risk taker so I always doubted my abilities, especially when it came to starting something new. I used to set very high standards for myself and if I didn't achieve at that level, I'd put myself down and doubt myself continuously. This just spiraled out of control and I really did not know where to turn. Kate gave me the tools to set realistic goals with time parameters so that I could hold myself accountable.

I set a health goal for myself because I'd had an emergency back operation. I was very busy at work so had no time to exercise. My job involved socializing on a regular basis which meant lots of eating and drinking. These were all just excuses that I continued to use and they were stopping me from being the healthy person I wanted to be. Once I realized this I made some decisions and set some goals.

The first was to find a personal trainer, and then I scheduled time in my diary for sessions and was unapologetic about fitting these personal appointments between my work appointments. I made it clear to my family and friends that I wanted to lose weight and become healthy. I didn't want to be on a constant diet worrying about food all the time so I tried a few programs, took the advice of my trainer and slowly started to see the results.

I also found an online health coach and slowly achieved even better results. When I plateaued I made a plan to change this by signing up for a 12-week body transformation challenge. I took it day by day, week by week, incorporating the tools that Kate gave me to keep going. I put together a health vision board and stuck it up on my mirror. This helped to motivate me. I could see what I wanted to become! I spoke to myself every day using positive reinforcements until my goal was manifested. I came second in the challenge and felt so proud of myself.

I realized that it was okay to take my time and to try a different approach if the current approach was not working. It doesn't have to happen first time around. Patience, persistence and planning changed this area of my life.

The second part of my life that needed some serious work was linked to my work situation. The company I worked for merged with a competitor and that is when my life turned upside down. Because of my self-limiting beliefs I could not bring myself to deal with the people and situation that made my life feel miserable. Although this was a very depressing stage of my life, it showed me that I actually needed a full shift in the work aspect of my life.

I realized that I wanted to do something different and be my own boss. I have always been a creative person but due to the nature of my job I was not able to use my creative abilities, which is partly what lead to my unhappiness in the corporate world.

Even with all my work with Kate, I continued to be miserable and had built up so much resentment and self-doubt that I was paralyzed. It was so frustrating. I blamed everybody and anything for my situation and it started having a huge negative impact on my family life.

It was at this stage that Kate was planning an Ignite Your Life retreat in Mauritius. I just knew that I had to go and be part of it. It was the best personal investment that I have made in a very long time. As a mom, partner, colleague, sister, daughter and employee, life can sometimes take over and you forget to just breathe. This retreat gave me the time and space to be with me.

I cannot describe how I felt waking up each day in a positive state. We started off every day with yoga on the beach, followed by a short meditation and then a day filled with learning life lessons and so much laughter. It was during these five special days that I actually realized that my self-limiting beliefs and unrealistic fears were causing so much pain in my life. We smashed pieces of wood in half with our bare hands threw coconuts into the sea to face our fears and reduce them forever. Kate gave us tools to use each day to approach how we deal with ourselves and, in particular, how we set new goals and follow through. I created the most awesome vision board, which is still on my mirror today as a reminder of what I want to achieve in my life.

It is through these five days that I started to see the light. I made peace with the people who I thought were keeping me from being happy. I have also now embarked on a process to start my own business – and it is identical to my vision board! I am so motivated to achieve this one very important goal in my life. I want to leave a legacy for my son and now I know that it is possible. I will manifest this vision. I know it will take hard work, dedication, patience (with myself), follow-through and continuous positive reinforcement. Thanks to Kate I now have the tools to achieve my dream. She definitely helped me to ignite my life. She is my angel and I will forever be indebted to her for sharing this positive life experience.

VH

I FACED MY FEARS

I was lucky to have met Kate Emmerson in Warsaw at an Ignite Your Life workshop. Since that day my life has never been the same. My journey of self-discovery and facing my fears was fired up with a welcome kick and jumpstart. Kate has been a true inspiration in my life; her incredible spirit, strength, humor, vision and, most importantly, humanity have helped me to wake up and see the light again – and even the thunder!

The hardest part for me was dealing with my limiting beliefs as my self-esteem was pretty low before I met Kate. Also, due to my non-assertive character, I found it difficult to put myself first without feeling guilty all the time. Facing my fears was another big issue in my life, but with Kate's tools and incredible insights I felt I was ready to move on in my life and finally face my fears.

After Kate's workshop in Warsaw, my incredible journey began and I made sure that our paths crossed again. Just a few months later, Kate came to Cyprus for workshops. This time I felt my life shifting as I made the short-term goals that she strongly encouraged me to do, along with re-evaluating them every few weeks. This has changed my life! I landed a position I never expected. My house is almost clutter free and I feel determined to keep on going as I still have a lot more exciting plans on my agenda. Tranquility, happiness and living lighter were waiting for me on the other side of all that work.

Nobody is perfect and life is a continuous flow with ups and downs. However I now stop myself from dwelling and procrastinating, and try to shift my feelings and remember Kate's beautiful voice and "va va voom" to give myself a kick in the behind.

I sometimes go off course and repeat my mistakes, mainly feeling guilty, when I try to be more assertive. Luckily my inner voice gets a wake-up call from Kate and I come back on track.
Eleni Ellinas

BACK ON TRACK

While I was on maternity leave in 2014, after having my second child, I felt the urge to get my life back in order. At the time, we were renovating our house and staying with my parents and I felt overwhelmed by the many things on my to-do list, which I just was not getting done.

There were huge chunks of my life that I hadn't really paid much attention to since starting a family two years earlier. I was also in the process of returning to my work in a professional services firm and trying to figure out how to achieve some sort of work-life balance. I battled with the fact that I didn't feel successful either as a mom or in my career and the situation was causing me a lot of stress.

Becoming overwhelmed in my professional and personal life has been a challenge I have faced over and over again; and in that situation I would typically procrastinate, give up and not know how to get myself back on track. Looking back now, maybe feeling overwhelmed was a way of disempowering and sabotaging myself from moving forward in my life.

Working with the support of Kate, I tackled my backlog of work and personal stuff, things I had been putting off, to free up my energy. I realized that I didn't actually have appropriate (or any) systems to deal with my workflow and emails, for example. Some of my stress at work was because I was not good at setting clear expectations upfront for my team, and I ended up spending a lot of time fixing the mess afterwards. I have been working on these areas and have been steadily improving, although I still have some way to go.

I identified some of the factors that contributed to my being overwhelmed. One of them was the sense that I had to get everything done immediately. I wanted instant gratification. For example, it stressed me out that my house, after moving back in, was not yet furnished nicely and I wished that somebody would just wave a magic wand and transform my home into a beautiful, uncluttered, organized space.

Through the process with Kate, I have learned that I can work systematically on a project and allow myself the space and time to get it done. I have also done a Cycle of Life exercise to start paying attention to those areas of my life that I feel I have been neglecting. I now know that success doesn't come overnight. It needs to be worked on consistently and the important thing is not to beat myself up every time something doesn't work out perfectly, but rather to pick myself up, use my tools and try again.
Ulrike

LIVING WITH AUTHENTICITY

Working with "kick-ass" Kate may be a (pleasant) shock to the system. Your life my never be the same again, but you will not regret living large, being light and ignited.

My journey with Kate started almost a decade ago and I am still inspired by this dynamic deva. Kate is a true reflection of her brand, energetic, witty, enthusiastic, funky, no nonsense, deeply caring, and passionate about her calling to transform South Africa and the world, one life, one home and one business at a time.

She is one of the most authentic people I know, which is the part of our work that I find most valuable in living a life true to myself. In society we are all molded by pressure and expectations to some extent and it is easy to forget how we really want to live. Not only does Kate guide and teach you the skills to re-discover your real self, but her authenticity gently rubs off while you create the life you always wanted.

I started with personal coaching before doing Kate's courses. Years later, I am still using the skills because they are practical and work for me. One of my worst enemies, like many of us, is self-sabotage. As soon as I became aware of it, I quickly learned to recognize when I am sabotaging myself in any area of my life. I feel self-empowered every time I apply the simple yet effective skill to bust sabotage immediately. It works because it is a tool Kate and I designed together for me personally.

As you may know from your own experience, I find that working on myself and improving my quality of life is an invaluable investment, but also a work in progress. Once you commit to the process and experience the wonderful joys of the results, rewards and sense of achievement, you will be hooked. You will be shifting, growing, daring, relapsing sometimes but always bouncing back, dreaming, living lighter and loving your life.

This journey is not for sissies. I can confidently say, whether it is through a course, book, workshop or personal coaching, Kate is the best of the best. She's hard-core (believe me, really hard-core) but she cares too much to leave you the way you began. Her steadfast commitment, experience, knowledge, ability and passion to enrich people's lives puts her in a league of her own.

I am forever grateful for the privilege of working with this world-class expert and the way our process changed my life.

Marlize Pretorius

MY DREAM LIFE

Kate Emmerson has probably had the biggest influence in my personal development and the space where I am now, which is very happy, and full of significance, meaning, creativity and contribution. When I look back over my life journey I can clearly identify how Kate provided that vital pull that put me on the path that eventually changed my life for the better, forever.

I am a reasonably intelligent and creative person, brought on by my curiosity and the fact that I studied and worked in the civil and structural engineering field. But depending on the company in which I found myself, I was mostly shy and withdrawn. This created huge problems for me in my work environment. Because of my responsibility as a project engineering design draftsman, I regularly had to attend project meetings with engineers, building contractors and the like to discuss how we could do the work better. I would always prepare well for these meetings, with some good written proposals for the success of a project. But once the meeting started, I would be agonizingly afraid of speaking. Almost always, someone else would suggest similar or inferior solutions than the ones I had come up with but not shared, and they would get all the accolades and acknowledgment. I allowed this to happen to me for many years in my career. I also allowed it to happen in my sporting and social life.

I knew that it was a confidence thing. I had the ability and the capacity to do well, but I just had to get off my butt and do it. I kept on searching and working on it, albeit slowly and sometimes grudgingly. I attended many personal development courses. Many of them were good, and expensive, and they helped improve some areas of my life. But with hindsight I know that I just wasn't integrating the lessons I learned and that I was repeating the same mistakes.

Then I heard about Kick-Ass Kate. She promised to do "how to get your groove back" (HTGYGB) work with me. Our first meeting was a one-to-one personal session in Cape Town. I was immediately drawn to her authentic interest in helping me out of my rut. She listened intently to me as she drew the conversation out of me. Her questions got me so excited to share much more than I had ever cared to share with anyone.

As we worked together, whenever I got stuck with an assignment she would encourage me with Brian Tracey's "Eat the Frog" philosophy.

The most engaging part of the HTYGB program was the Cycle of Life exercise. It really helped me to look at my life as a whole and then to examine every slice of it and how each one affected the other – and my entire life. It helped me to create goals and an action plan for each slice of life. I haven't achieved all my goals yet, but I'm in a much better space emotionally. It is the best self-awareness tool I've ever come across. It has definitely played a huge role in my personal growth and development.

After HTYGB, Kate has stayed in touch with me. We had another one-to-one coaching session and I joined a mastermind group with other participants of the HTYGB program. Group members got together for an online chat from 7 a.m. to 8 a.m. every Monday, so we could share our experiences. We work together to help each other overcome challenges and achieve their goals. It is a great model of group learning and teaching through our own personal experiences and has helped me understand that other people like me are going through the same pain and joy of growth.

A highlight of my association with Kate is when she got me to attend what I consider to be my breakthrough workshop experience, which was presented by Nick Williams, owner of The Inspirational Learning Company. Kate invited him to present his legendary Becoming an Inspired Entrepreneur one-day workshop in Cape Town. The information shared by Nick and proud host Kate has stayed with me to this day.

Kate's encouragement and motivation keeps on feeding my soul and firing up my desire to grow and share my gift. She has taught me how to care for myself first so that I can truly care for my fellow human beings.

Kate, thanks so much for once again challenging me to relive and experience the journey that I've traveled with you. It has been a long and difficult road, filled with the pain and joy of growth. But it has brought me to a place where I know what it's like to live light and live large.

Thanks to Kate I am now living my dream and fulfilling my calling. I am a superbalist (someone who consciously chooses to be superb in everything) and emotional intelligence coach. I am sharing my gift at every opportunity, in schools, youth groups, sports clubs, rehabilitation centers and prisons. The best part of sharing my gift is that I love what I do. And the more I share my gift, the better and bigger it becomes.

Kate, I remain forever grateful to you for illuminating my path at a time when I needed it most. Thanks so much for kicking my ass when I slowed down on our journey. Thanks for kissing it better when you saw that I needed it most.

Mike Fraser

GO WELL AND BE BLESSED

In parting, allow me to share a poem I wrote when I was 26.
Be blessed on your journey.

BEYOND DUALITY
It's feeling reliable & strong whilst our bodies are weary
Wise even when asking foolish questions
Stable yet moving along at top speed
Knowing abundance when the bank balance glares zero
Remaining compassionate in the face of a gun barrel
It's about creating & simultaneously destroying
Remembering death is really a new beginning
Allowing joy to flow through all the tears
Teaching alongside the blessing of learning
Feeling peace amidst total rampant chaos
Accessing serenity through the sorrow of grief
Spiraling beyond duality shifts us from thinking we are separate…
then remembering we are one
Being ALL OF ME & ALL OF YOU &
remembering US as being part of ALL THAT IS
AKWE

Diagrams and worksheets

DIAGRAM 1

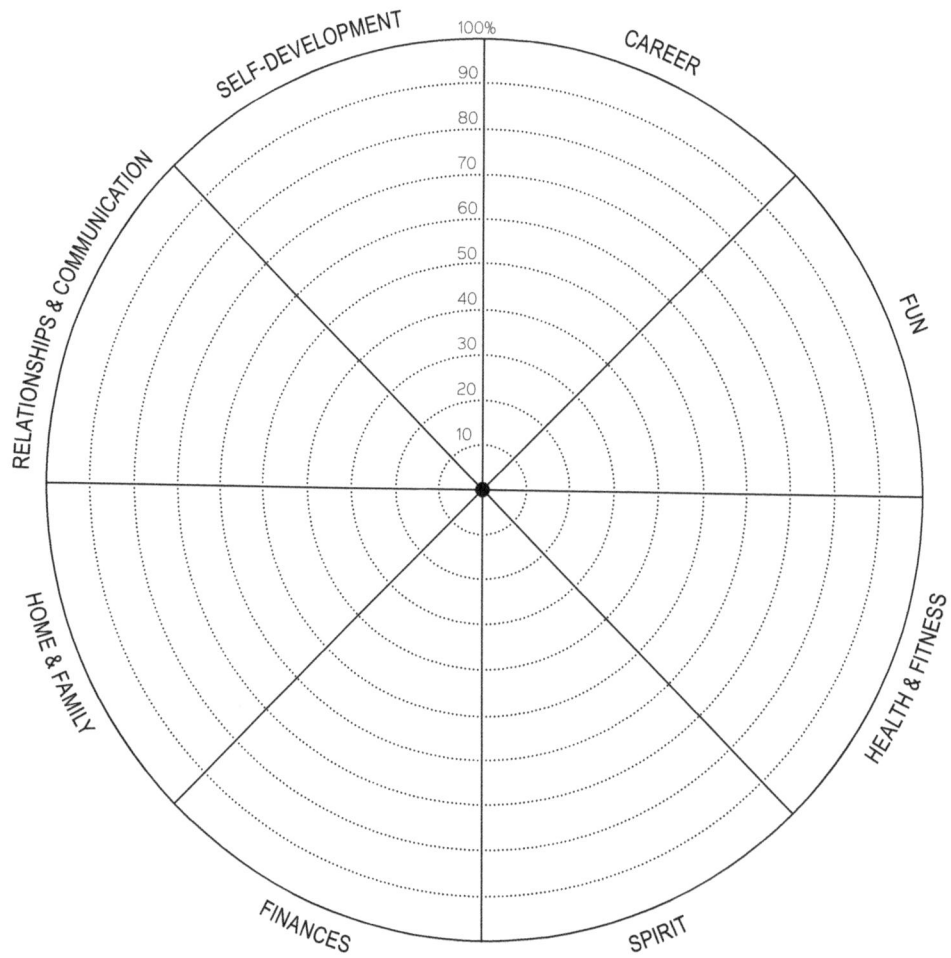

DIAGRAM 2

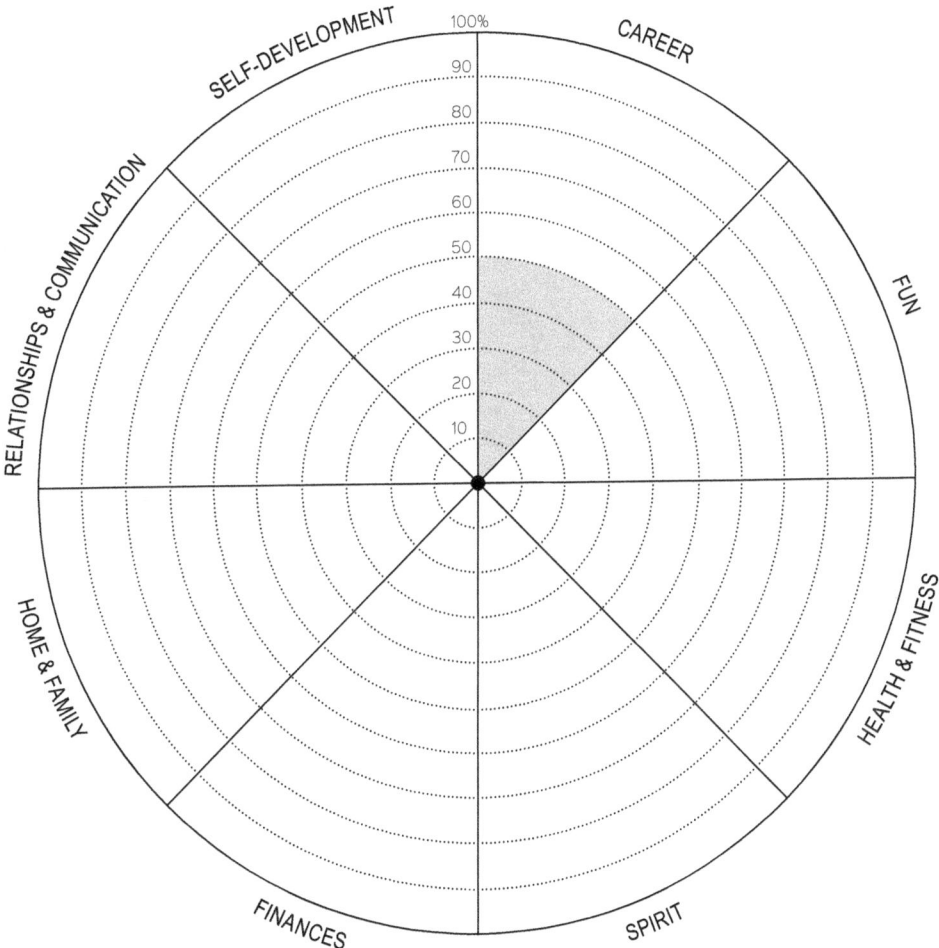

Diagrams and worksheets 147

DIAGRAM 3

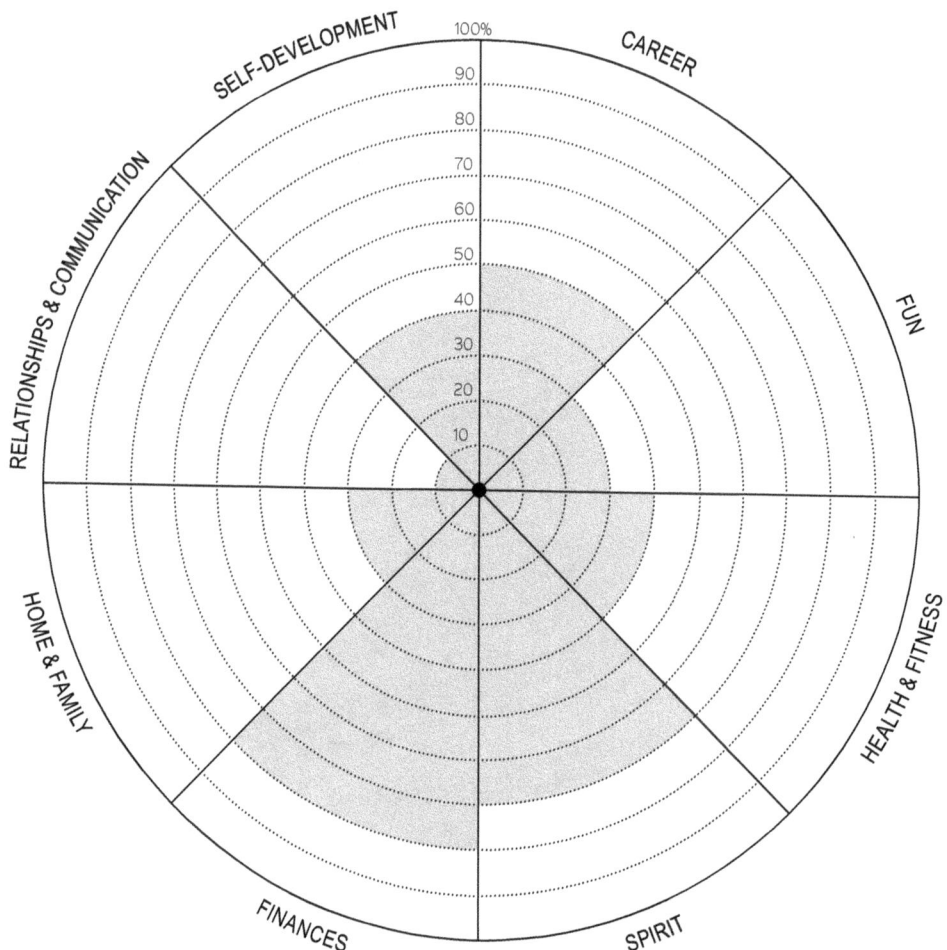

DIAGRAM 4

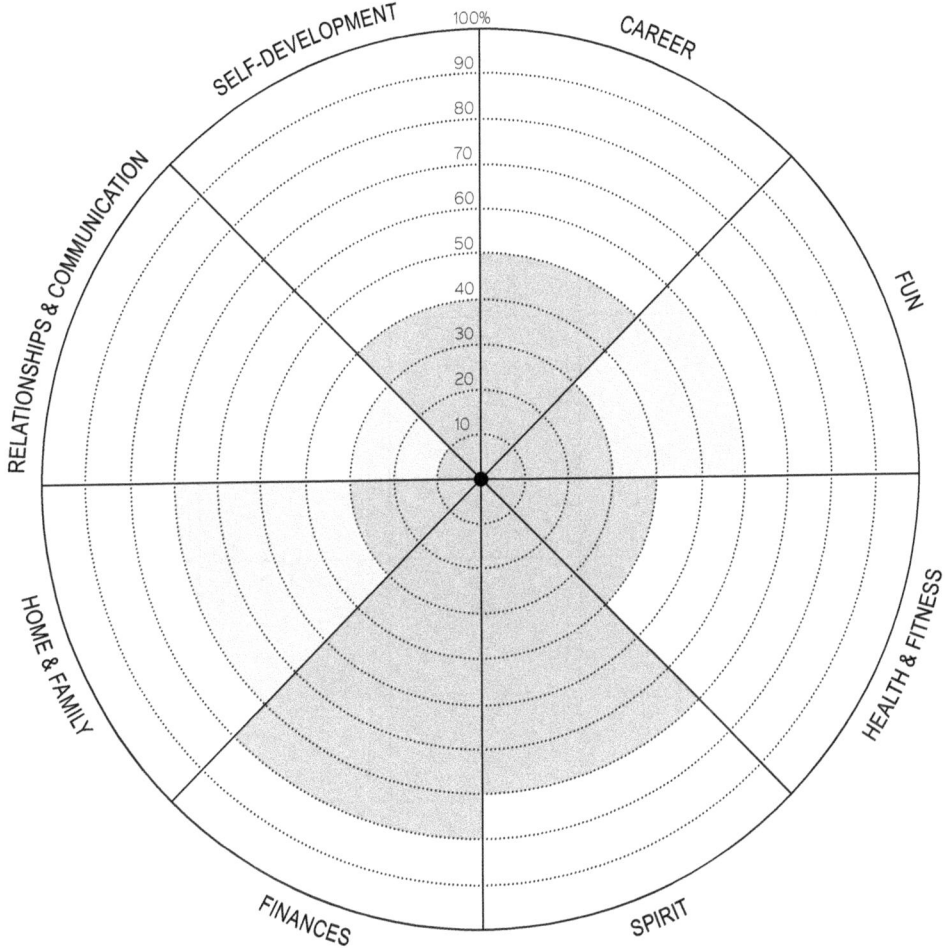

ACTION PLAN 1

WEEK ENDING:	MON ACTIONS	TUE ACTIONS	WED ACTIONS	THU ACTIONS
GOAL 1				
GOAL 2				
GOAL 3				
Daily Gratitude Journaling				
Fire Rating 1-10 & action				

I am positively shifting these three areas of life. I know that I am ultimately in control of my life, my thoughts and my choices. I make empowered choices in line with what is important to me. I have the support I need and the ability to succeed.

FRI ACTIONS	SAT ACTIONS	SUN ACTIONS	REWARD!

ACTION PLAN 2

WEEK ENDING:	MON ACTIONS	TUE ACTIONS	WED ACTIONS	THU ACTIONS
GOAL 1				
GOAL 2				
GOAL 3				
Daily Gratitude Journaling				
Fire Rating 1-10 & action				
Healthy boundaries				

My new positive beliefs I created to support me achieving the above goals are:

1. ....

2. ....

3. ....

FRI ACTIONS	SAT ACTIONS	SUN ACTIONS	REWARD!

4. ....
5. ....
6. ....
7. ....

ACTION PLAN 3

WEEK ENDING:	MON ACTIONS	TUE ACTIONS	WED ACTIONS	THU ACTIONS
GOAL 1				
GOAL 2				
GOAL 3				
Daily Gratitude Journaling				
Fire Rating 1-10 & action				
Healthy boundaries				

I am willing to increase my commitment this week by:

....

My positive beliefs to support me achieving the above goals:

....

FRI ACTIONS	SAT ACTIONS	SUN ACTIONS	REWARD!

My top three values:

....
....
....
....

ACTION PLAN 4

THE LAST PUSH UP THE HILL!	Day 1	Day 2	Day 3	Day 4
GOAL 1:				
Original %				
Today's %				
I am just …% short of my 5 week goal of …%				
GOAL 2:				
Original %				
Today's %				
I am just …% short of my goal of …%				
GOAL 3:				
Original %				
Today's %				
I am just …% short of my goal of …%				
Gratitude Journaling				
Fire Rating 1-10 & action				

What am I willing to do to ensure I reach my goals this week?

....

....

....

Who can help me?	The boldest thing I will do to achieve this goal!	Conversations to have or boundaries to stick to!	BIG REWARD!!!!

I value myself and my life and my goals and will do what it takes to reach them…

....
....
....

FURTHER READING

These are some of the books that have guided me on my personal path and helped me face life and the ups and downs we all go through.

Branson, Richard. *Screw it, Let's do it* (Virgin Books, 2010)
Buckingham, M. and Clifton, D. *Now. Discover Your Strengths* (Pocket Books, 2004)
Buckingham, Marcus. *Go put your Strengths to Work* (Simon & Schuster, 2007)
Burchard, Brendon. *The Millionaire Messenger* (Free Press, 2011)
Canfield, Jack. *The Success Principles* (HarperCollins Publishers, 2005)
Ferriss, Tim. *The 4-hour Work Week* (Crown Publishers, 2007)
Gyatso, Geshe Kelsang. *Introduction to Buddhism* (Tharpa Publications, 1992)
Harrold, Fiona. *Be Your own Life Coach* (Hodder & Stoughton, 2000)
Harrold, Fiona. *The 10-minute Life Coach* (Hodder & Stoughton, 2002)
Hawkins, David. *Letting Go* (Hay House Inc, 2012)
Hay, Louise. *You can Heal your Life* (Hay House, 1985)
Hendrix, Harville. *Getting the Love you Want* (Harper Perennial, 1991)
Hendrix, Harville. *Keeping the Love you Find* (Pocket Books, 1995)
Hendrix, Harville and Hunt, Helen. *Receiving Love* (Simon & Schuster, 2005)
Hicks, Esther and Jerry. *Ask and it is Given* (Hay House Inc, 2004)
Hicks, Esther and Jerry. *The Vortex* (Hay House Inc, 2009)
Huffington, Ariana. *Thrive* (Harmony Books, 2014)
Katie, Byron. *Loving what Is* (Harmony Books, 2002)
Kingston, Karen. *Clear your Clutter with Feng Shui* (Piatkus, 1998)
Kingston, Karen. *Creating Sacred Space with Feng Shui* (Piatkus, 1996)
Lerner, Harriet. *The Dance of Anger* (Perennial Currents: 20th Anniversary Edition, May 2005)
Lerner, Harriet. *The Dance of Intimacy* (William Morrow Paperbacks: Reprint edition, March 1990)
Linn, Denise. *Soul Coaching* (Hay House Inc, 2003)
Myss, Caroline. *Anatomy of the Spirit* (Three Rivers Press, 1997)
Myss, Caroline. *Why People don't Heal and How they Can* (Three Rivers Press, 1988)
Myss Caroline. *Invisible Acts of Power* (Simon & Schuster, 2004)
Orman, Suze. *The 9 Steps to Financial Freedom* (Crown Business, 2006)
Parkin, John C. *F**K it Therapy* (Hay House Inc, 2012)
Ruiz, Don Miguel. *The Four Agreements* (Amber-Allen Publishing, 1997)
Ruiz, Don Miguel. *The Mastery of Love* (Amber-Allen Publishing, 1999)
Teversham, Liesel. *The Upside of Saying No* (Kima Global Publishers, 2012)
Tracy, Brian. *Eat that frog!* (Berret-Koehler Publishers, 2007)
Veenman, Warren and Eichhorst, Sally. *Dare to Succeed* (Reach Publishers, 2013)
Walsh, Peter. *It's all too Much* (Free Press, 2007)
Williams, Nick. *Resisting your Soul* (Balloon View, 2011)
Williams, Nick. *The Work we were Born to Do* (Element Books, 1999)

REVIEWS OF *DITCH YOUR GLITCH*

Like a good friend who tells you hard truths, Kate takes you firmly by the hand and guides you on a challenging, life-changing journey. Bravely revealing her own story throughout, she gives you the courage to face your glitches and heal past hurts ... with the take-charge tools you need to transform your life.
Fiona Davern, executive editor at Destiny magazine. South Africa

The pages of Ditch your Glitch *hold a wisdom and energy that is hard to express. Kate's authenticity, complimented by her passion, will help you create remarkable shifts. I have attended a self-development growth club for a year and I find that Kate's book encapsulates most of what I have learnt.*
Celynn Erasmus, professional speaker, registered dietician, author, passionate foodie. South Africa

Kate Emmerson takes you on a step-by-step process beyond your comfort zone to honestly face aspects of yourself and your life that you may not be comfortable with and to realise that success in your life starts with you ... sharing her journey with the reader, making the lessons believable and achievable. This book will challenge you to get started on a whole new path to success and fulfilment with a renewed zest. I know that's what it did for me.
Colleen Larsen, CE: Business Engage. South Africa

Ditch your Glitch encourages us to look deep into our core to find our magnificence. [It] guides us to ditch our glitch with easy to follow steps and enlightening examples. Kate bravely shares her own story and exposes her glitches, showing that she doesn't just talk the talk; she walks the walk.
Carol Scibelli, author. New York.

Kate has beautifully blended her own personal experiences, her clients' examples and practical exercises that walk you through each step of the way, along with holding you accountable so you are gently pushed towards your goals that you have defined. If you're ready to move forward in life, this book will help you do just that.
Lori Park, Angel Intuitive, Chicago

... a book that you won't be able to put down! It truly will help you shift your life and perspective ... will inspire you to take action today! Kate's book will motivate you to be your very best self and will also help you to reach unlimited potential!
Beth Bracaglia, Chief Simplicity Officer of Simply Organized, creator of Beth Bracaglia's Simply Inspired. Ellicott City

Ditch your Glitch is a meaningful and real step-by-step transformational work-out that, if you remain true to your commitments, will bring about the desired changes in your life. I feel like I am thriving more than before I read this book. I have moved from mere existence to truly living. And you too can!
Alex Granger, CEO: The Possibility of YOU, professional speaker, author. South Africa

... a practical step-by-step guide to creating personal transformation by understanding and addressing those things that are holding you back from creating a better, more fulfilled life. [Kate] doesn't tell you how to do it – she shows you. By using her own personal journey as insightful examples, she makes you feel as if she is there with you in this easy to follow, actionable, transformative and very readable book.
Tessa Graham, Capturing Brilliance, Creating Brands, Building Businesses. South Africa

... a truly inspiring book [that] helped me finally get over my issues with forgiving, which was the hardest part. I am now in control of my emotions and I will not allow people to use and abuse me anymore. I have taken action on all aspects of my life and it feels great. I will buy this book for all my family members and my friends who I know will benefit from it.
Yolanda Duvenhage, A brave woman reclaiming her life

Was I surprised when she went straight to my glitch at the beginning of the book, describing it in finest detail. It made me pay attention to what followed. My thinking shifted in the most powerful way. Forever.
Melanie Brummer, entrepreneur, author. South Africa

... Ditch Your Glitch is witty, down to earth, personal, full of great reminders, and my favourite part is that her book embodies Kate's spunk, spark, energy as a person and her same zeal for life.
Carly Alyssa Thorne, author, speaker, producer, director. UK